A Pictorial History TUBAC
WHERE ART AND HISTORY MEET

By Mark Bollin and Mary Bingham

Copyright© 2006 by *The Green Valley News and Sun*
Published by *The Green Valley News and Sun*
All rights reserved. No part of this book may be reproduced, stored in a retrieval system or transmitted in any form or by any means, electronic, mechanical, photocopying, recording or otherwise, without prior written permission of the copyright owner or the publisher.
ISBN: 1-59725-057-0 • First Edition • 1,250 copies
Every attempt was made to secure permission for captions and photographs, and to credit our sources accurately.
Published by Pediment Publishing, a division of The Pediment Group, Inc. www.pediment.com

TABLE OF CONTENTS

Introduction 4

Acknowledgments 5

Tubac the Old Town 6

Historic Parks 23

Celebrations 43

Old Buildings With New Faces 59

Where They Lived and Worked 78

Recreation 97

Other Places of Interest 107

Highways & Byways 112

Index 117

INTRODUCTION

There is a special tone, a special feel that surrounds Tubac. Artists came for the unique light that the southwestern sun splashes over the town and into their studios. Ranchers and farmers were drawn to the nurturing waters of the Santa Cruz River and the fertile soils of the river valley. Since Padre Eusebio Francisco Kino ventured into the Santa Cruz River Valley in 1691 in search of souls to save, Tubac has endured cycles of destruction and desolation only to recover and grow again into the unique community that it is today.

This first volume is meant to be a pictorial collection of the people and places that have made Tubac and the surrounding areas what they were in the late 1700's, and what they are today. Working with photographs from historical repositories such as the Tubac Historical Society, the Tumacacori National Historical Park, the Tubac Presidio State Historic Park, as well as many private sources, we hope this book begins to capture the special ambiance that is Tubac ... where art and history meet.

Mark Bollin
Marketing Director
Green Valley News & Sun

ACKNOWLEDGMENTS

As with any ambitious project, it is extraordinary people and organizations that contribute their talent, knowledge, and passion to the pages that lay before you. Special recognition is given to Mary Bingham of the Tubac Historical Society whose knowledge and assistance helped make publishing this book possible. The Green Valley News & Sun recognizes and appreciates the following for their contribution to this book:

Tubac Historical Society
Mary Bingham
Dan Judkins
Irene Deaton

Tubac Golf Resort
Ron Allred
Mark Scheller

Tubac and Green Valley
Bunny Hanson
Lucy Robling
John Montgomery
Sally Barter
Bob Johnson
Olivia Cabot
Olga Leone
Brian & Kathleen Vandervoet

Dorn Homes
David Grounds

King Ranch
R. Joe King

Brasher Real Estate
Gary Brasher
Carl Bosse

Tumacacori National Historic Park
Roy Simpson

Tubac Presidio State Park
Joe Martinez

Green Valley News & Sun
Mario Aguilar

Santa Cruz Chili Factory
Jean England Neubauer

Tucson
Virginia Cullin Roberts

Tubac Center of the Arts
Josie De Falla

Green Valley News & Sun
Pam Mox
Mark Bollin

Tucson Musem of Art
Jill Provan

Cow Palace
Frank Bertalino

Wisdom's Café
Herb Wisdom

Will Rogers Memorial Museum
Steve Gragert

Truly Nolen, Inc.
Scott Nolen

TUBAC THE OLD TOWN

Tubac's quaint streets and alleys connecting homes and studios of working artists with local merchants reveal only a hint of its past. In viewing the photographs, maps and lithographs that follow, we hope a sense of the old Tubac can be felt, imagined and remembered.

During Tubac's first three centuries three men had a major influence on the history and character of the village. They were Father Eusebio Francisco Kino, Captain Juan Bautista de Anza and Charles D. Poston.

Father Eusebio Francisco Kino, the Jesuit missionary and explorer established more than twenty missions in the Pimería Alta. Three missions were located near Tubac including: San Cayetano de Tumacácori (1691), Los Santos Angeles de Guevavi (1691) and San Xavier del Bac (1692). Tubac soon became a ranchería (farming community) in support of Tumacácori.

Juan Bautista de Anza was the second commandant of the Spanish royal presidio or fort of San Ignacio de Tubac from 1760 to 1776. During his last three years in Tubac, Anza headed up an exploratory expedition establishing an overland route to California and a second expedition leading a party of over 300 colonists to establish the city of San Francisco. During this time, Tubac was the final outpost for recruiting and provisioning before crossing the desert. Anza Days commemorates the man and his exploits.

Charles D. Poston from Kentucky, an adventurer and speculator, with the help of Raphael Pumpelly, Samuel Heintzelman, William Wrightson, Horace Grosvenor, and a hosts of others, established Tubac as a major center of mining as early as 1856. By 1859 it was the largest town in Doña Ana County, New Mexico Territory, with approximately 120 citizens. Tubac would not see a population to match that count until more than a century later.

TERRITORIAL TUBAC

ABOVE: This is one of the most familiar images of early Tubac and was drawn by J. Ross Browne. It was sketched in 1864 while on an inspection tour of Poston's mining interests in the Tubac area during the Civil War. On the left is the former Tubac presidio used by Poston to house the headquarters of his Sonora Exploring and Mining Co. By 1864 the presidio was once again a military fort under the command of the U. S. Army. Santa Gertrudis Chapel built by presidial Captain Juan Bautista de Anza (c. 1766) can be seen in the center. The building on the right is near the present location of the Hugh Cabot Studios-Gallery. *Courtesy Tubac Historical Society*

LEFT: John Ross Browne was a world traveler, illustrator and artist. It is fitting that he was one of the first artists to sketch Tubac. His popular articles, "A Tour Through Arizona" appeared in the *Harper's New Monthly Magazine* and were later published in book form. *Courtesy Tubac Historical Soceity*

LEFT: Charles DeBrille Poston, the self proclaimed "Father of Arizona," came to Tubac soon after the Gadsden Purchase of 1853. He quickly set up mining operations at the old Salero Mine and built the Hacienda de Santa Rita facilities to house the workers and process ore.
Source: History of Arizona by Thomas E. Farish. The Filmer Brothers Electrotype Co., 1915-1918

LEFT & BELOW: "Valley of the Santa Cruz" as viewed from near the present day border looking into Nogales, Sonora, Mexico and "Early View of Tubac and the Santa Rita Mountains" as seen from the southwest side of the valley are attributed to the talented illustrator and surveyor, Charles Schuchard. Both images were sketched while a member of the 1854 Texas Western Railroad survey team. Schuchard returned to the Tubac area after completing the survey. We have early explorers, surveyor and diarists to thank for the images we have today.   *Courtesy Mary Bingham*

ABOVE: Old stage coach similar to the one barely visible in the photo to the right. *Courtesy Tumacácori National Historical Park*

RIGHT: Portion of an early stereo view of Tubac, circa 1870s. Building in background may be the old Glassman hotel which stood near the Rojas House. Note dog standing in the doorway of the building in foreground.
Courtesy Tumacácori National Historical Park

OTERO LAND GRANT

The first Spanish land grant in Arizona was awarded to Don Toribio de Otero on January 10, 1789. Held by the Oteros for nearly 140 years, a few of the original buildings still exist including the family home, silos and stables. Today, the property is owned by the Tubac Golf Resort.

Courtesy Barbara Ruppman Collection, Tubac Historical Society

Otero Family Brands

First Otero Brand

José Tiburcio Otero

Sabino Otero

Teofilo Otero

Altered SO Brand

Menager & Otero

Courtesy Shaw Kinsley

ABOVE: Ana Marie Coenen (1859-1946), a niece of Sabino Otero was the last Otero to live on the old Otero land grant.
Courtesy Tubac Historical Society

LEFT: Sabino Otero (1846-1914), great-grandson of Toribio, was the most successful of the Otero family with extensive interests in ranching, freighting and real estate in Tubac and Tucson. Otero was the link between Tubac's Spanish & Mexican colonial past and the American territorial period. His legacy and that of the Otero family continues to this day.   *Courtesy Tubac Historical Society*

KING RANCH

ABOVE: The old King ranch, now owned by the Peachey family, dates back to the 1860s when Joseph King, a Portuguese master mariner, arrived with William Wrightson's 1864 survey team to map the amended Baca Float No. 3. The twelve square-mile claim included the famous Salero Mine. King helped to build the road to Salero and many of the buildings at the Hacienda de Santa Rita before settling down. Plans for the Aztec, Truman and Tyndall Mining Districts (see map page 14) were drawn up at his ranch house.
Courtesy R. Joe King

RIGHT: Sign marking the St. Joseph's Cemetery. *Courtesy R. Joe King*

BELOW: Graves of the Portuguese mariner, Joseph King (1828-1912), his wife Trinidad Ramirez de King (1860-1925), and daughter-in-law, Margarita Andrade King (1874-1913). *Courtesy R. Joe King*

LEFT: Joe King, II (1889-1982) was 29 years-old when he enlisted in the U.S. Army to serve in WWI. He was the third son of the Portuguese mariner. *Courtesy R. Joe King*

RIGHT Wedding picture of Joseph King, II, and wife Maria Amparo Tapia on their wedding day in 1922. A generation earlier, King's father and mother were married by T. Lillie Mercer in Tubac.
Courtesy R. Joe King

BELOW: September 19, 1917, Joseph King II (front row, fourth from left), and forty-two other men were inducted into Company B, 340th Field Artillery. They boarded the train in Nogales taking them to Camp Funston, Kansas for basic training. King would later fight in the Meuse-Argonne Offensive of 1918.   *Courtesy R. Joe King*

SALERO MINE/HACIENDA DE SANTA RITA

HACIENDA OF THE SANTA RITA MINING COMPANY.

LEFT: This sketch of the "Hacienda de Santa Rita Mining Company" was done by J. Ross Browne in 1864. Originally an old Jesuit mine, Salero was the first mining site claimed by Poston and his partners.
Source: "Harper's New Monthly," March 1865.

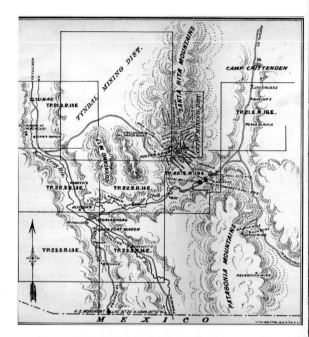

RIGHT: Map of the township of the Santa Rita including the Aztec and Tyndall Mining Districts. This map appeared in *Hinton's Handbook to Arizona* 1877. *Courtesy Tubac Historical Society*

BELOW: In 2004 the best-preserved stone wall at the Hacienda de Santa Rita still stands some ten feet high. *Courtesy Dan Judkins*

ABOVE: Sign posted at the entrance to the Salero Ranch warns: "2 employees were murdered here. It is dangerous for you to carry firearms."
Courtesy Dan Judkins

RIGHT: One of several graves located near the old hacienda site. *Courtesy Dan Judkins*

EL TORREÓN RANCH

ABOVE: Only known picture of El Torreón (c. 1900) a ranch owned by Ynez Andrade and wife Mariana. The family was evicted from their property in 1914 as a result of the Baca Float No. 3 decision along with at least 39 other families. *Courtesy Eddie and Peggy Andrade Collection, Tubac Historical Society*

LEFT: Mariana Marquez de Andrade (1846-1935), wife of Ynez Andrade. Photo taken towards the end of her life.
Courtesy Eddie and Peggy Andrade Collection, Tubac Historical Society

RIGHT: Cayetano Andrade, son of Ynez and Mariana, was the Santa Cruz County constable for District #3 (Tubac) from 1907 to 1914. He was arrested while trying to harvest his crops from El Torreón shortly after the family was evicted. While in the Nogales jail he was fed with his own vegetables "laced with some kind of poison." He survived but went insane and died in the Arizona State Hospital in 1921.
Courtesy Eddie and Peggy Andrade Collection, Tubac Historical Society

A SERIES OF FOUR PHOTOS OF TUBAC TAKEN BY ROBERT H. FORBES ON MAY 16, 1915

LEFT: Building on right was the home of Forbes' mother-in-law, Larcena Pennington Page in 1864. It was the reason for his visit to Tubac on this day. Today the building is the Hugh Cabot Studios-Gallery. The first St. Ann's church is in the center and the 1885 Tubac schoolhouse can be seen on the left.
Courtesy Tumacácori National Historical Park

BELOW: View of Tubac, looking north from the old Tucson-Nogales Highway or Anza Trail. The building on the right was the Tully & Ochoa Store; on the left was Pie Allen's stand. The Acuña home was one of the buildings north of Tully & Ochoa. The Lowe House and Tubac post office are at the top of the hill.
Courtesy Tumacácori National Historical Park

RIGHT: Luis Acuña Gastellum, c. 1919, in front of his home on the old Anza Trail.
Courtesy Tubac Historical Society

TUBAC: WHERE ART & HISTORY MEET

ABOVE: Facing west on Calle Iglesia (formerly known as River Road & Church Street), St. Ann's Church with beams supporting the walls is located in the center. The church was severely damaged during the torrential winter storms of 1914-1915. Portions of the Lowe and Pennington adobes are on the right, with the Tubac Schoolhouse on the left. *Courtesy Tumacácori National Historical Park*

RIGHT: Looking east along Calle Iglesia, the Lowe house, store and post office are on the left. The home of Charles D. Poston (built c. 1856) is in the center. The sign reads: WE CARRY COMPLETE LINE BUILDERS HARDWARE; sash doors lime cement; plaster on roofing; --Building Supplys -- Lowest Prices --; J. D. Halstead Lumber Co.; Nogales, Ariz. *Courtesy Tumacácori National Historical Park*

FOUR WINDS RANCH

In the early 1930s, Robert J. Caren, foreman of Four Winds ranch in Tumacácori, photographed ranching operations for his family to remember. Above, the men are "driving steers into the corral where they wait to be weighed."
Courtesy Chary Peck Collection, Tubac Historical Society

RIGHT: "X marks the scales and O the corral where the cattle wait to be weighed."
Courtesy Chary Peck Collection, Tubac Historical SocietySociety

BELOW: "A close up of the steer being branded with a rope around his foot." *Courtesy Chary Peck Collection, Tubac Historical Society*

ABOVE: One of Caren's daughters on a pony.
Courtesy Chary Peck Collection, Tubac Historical Society

ABOVE: Local ranch owners, "Mr. Kearns, Mr. Steel & Mr. Bernett, watch Mexican cowboys." *Courtesy Chary Peck Collection, Tubac Historical Society*

RIGHT: "A steer is branded with a running iron." *Courtesy Chary Peck Collection, Tubac Historical Society*

RIGHT: "The rider had to leave his horse to hold this steer, as they were working so fast they didn't have enough men." *Courtesy Chary Peck Collection, Tubac Historical Society*

BELOW: A peddler selling wares in the Tubac area stops at Four Winds Ranch in the 1930s. *Courtesy Chary Peck Collection, Tubac Historical Society*

ABOVE & BELOW: Robert J. Caren is shown holding baby Chris on the ranch house porch and posing in the yard. *Courtesy Chary Peck Collection, Tubac Historical Society*

TUBAC IN THE 1920s

ABOVE: Town of Tubac, on the main highway between Tucson and Nogales, July 9, 1929. The main road renamed Main Street, had been moved to the west on what is now Burruel Street. *Courtesy Tumacácori National Historical Park*

LEFT: One of at least three stores in Tubac, c. 1924. This may be the store of Miguel B. Sinohui.
Courtesy Tumacácori National Historical Park

RIGHT: Looking north from the *barrio de Tubac* (c. 1920) the Cantina is in the foreground with Otero Community Hall, directly above the roofline. To the left is St. Ann's and the Tubac schoolhouse.
Courtesy Tumacácori National Historical Park

TUBAC IN 1970

BELOW: During the 20th Century, the Tucson-Nogales Highway moved west twice. The first move was to Main St. now known as Burruel St. The second move was to the present day East Frontage Rd. With the second move came new businesses such as The Tubac Inn, Hesselbarth Gallery, Tubac Art Center and Harwood Steigers. The Tubac Valley Country Club and Estates were just beginning to be developed.   *Courtesy Tubac Historical Society*

1. The Tubac Inn
2. Hesselbarth Gallery
3. Tubac Art Center
4. Harwood Steiger's Factory
5. Garrett/Roger's House
6. St. Ann's Church
7. Old Tubac Schoolhouse
8. Otero Community Hall
9. Poston's Territory House
10. Lowe House
11. Pennington House/Cabot Gallery
12. El Presidito
13. Tubac Cemetery
14. Tubac Valley Country Club & Estates
15. St. Ann's Parrish Hall.

HISTORIC PARKS

Tubac Presidio State Historic Park located in the heart of Tubac, began as the northernmost military outpost on the Spanish frontier of New Spain. Named the Presidio of San Ignacio de Tubac, it was established in 1752 to protect the small settlement of Tubac and the nearby missions of Tumacácori, Guevavi and San Xavier after the 1751 Pima Rebellion. Fifty *soldados de cuera* (leather jacketed soldiers) were garrisoned at the post until 1776 when they were relocated to the new presidio at Tucson.

Manned by Pima, Mexican and American troops over the next hundred years, the Tubac presidio fell into ruin at the beginning of the 20th century. Tubac citizens including William Morrow, Frank & Gay Griffin, Will & Collier Rogers, Jr. recognizing its historical importance campaigned to have it declared Arizona's first state park in 1958. Today, the Park facilities include the Old Tubac Schoolhouse, Rojas House, Otero Community Hall, Tubac Museum and picnic area.

Tumacácori National Historical Park, located three miles south of Tubac, was established as a National Monument in 1908 and a National Park in 1991.

The current Mission San José de Tumacácori was built by the Franciscans between 1800-1822. Foundations of an earlier Jesuit mission are still visible on the park grounds. However, the original mission, established by the Jesuit missionary Father Eusebio Francisco Kino in 1691, was named San Cayetano de Tumacácori, and was located on the east side of the Santa Cruz River. Kino never mentioned Tubac in his writings, but it is more than likely that he visited the village on many occasions.

ABOVE: Entrance to the Tubac Presidio State Historic Park, Arizona's first state park.
Courtesy Bob Johnson Collection, Tubac Historical Society

TUBAC PRESIDIO STATE HISTORIC PARK

ABOVE: Artist's concept of how Juan Bautista de Anza, second Captain of the Tubac Presidio may have looked.
"From the Archival Collections, Museum Collections Repository, Western Archeological and Conservation Center, National Park Service"

ABOVE: Earliest known photo of the Tubac Presidio, c. 1890.
Courtesy Tubac Presidio State Historic Park

RIGHT: Josef de Urrutia's map of Tubac drawn between December 1766 and January 1767. It is the earliest known map of Tubac showing the Rio de Tubac (Santa Cruz River), cultivated fields between the river and the acequia or canal, the roads to Tumacácori, Sonitac (near Patagonia), San Xavier del Bac and the Altar Valley.
Courtesy Tubac Historical Society

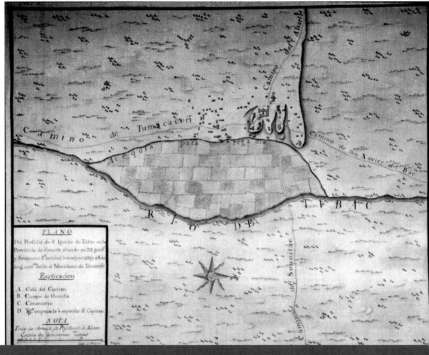

TUBAC SCHOOLHOUSE

LEFT: In 1885 the old Tubac Schoolhouse was funded by two notable local citizens--T. Lillie Mercer and Sabino Otero. Seen here in the early 1930s, the original one room adobe was also used for church services until St. Ann's Church and Otero Hall were built in 1912 & 1914. Additional classrooms were added in 1907 and teacher's apartments (the teacherage) in 1938. The community of Tubac saved the schoolhouse from demolition in 1969 adding it to the Tubac Presidio State Historic Park. A year later it was placed on the National Register of Historic Places.
Courtesy Chary Peck Collection, Tubac Historical Society

ABOVE: After renovation by the Tubac Historical Society the teacherage, on the west side of the Tubac Schoolhouse, was converted into the Elizabeth R. Brownell Library. This photo was taken at the 1984 dedication of the library. In 1995 the apartments were removed. *Courtesy Tubac Historical Society*

LEFT: Tubac class of 1929. The principal and teacher, Edwin P. Williams stands in the center between Refugio Valdez and Felix Olivas. Not all students are identified, but they include: Lucinda Sinouhi, Marie Ensley, Angelita Salcido, Adeline Rosenburg, Mercedes Sinouhi, Theresa Martinez, Anita Olivas, Maria Vega, Victoria Ochoa, Maria Moraga, Jesus Ochoa, Rosalia Vega, Isabel Sinouhi, Stella Rosenberg, Oralia Lowe, Roberto Lowe, Joe Otero, Jimmie Gastelum, Louis Gastelum and Pearl Parrish. Mr. Williams replaced Mr. Beattie (see photo page 26) in 1928. *Courtesy Tubac Historical Society*

ABOVE: Petition signed by Tubac citizens requesting establishment of a Tubac School District in December 1, 1876. Some signers include: Henry Glassman, Issac Goldberg, Dolores Pachecko, José María Figueroa, John T. Smith, Joseph King and James Peters. *Courtesy R. Joe King*

LEFT: Bob Barnacastle, manager of the Tubac Presidio State Historic Park from 1985 to 1996, is shown starting a fire in the antique potbelly stove in the Old Tubac Schoolhouse.
Courtesy Tubac Historical Society

RIGHT: Samuel H. Beattie, became the second teacher and principal of the Tubac school in 1914. He taught grades four and eight and took his students on field trips to the Santa Rita and Tumacácori Mountains. He retired in 1928.
Courtesy Tubac Historical Society

LEFT: Throughout the year, schools from southern Arizona bring classes to Tubac for a taste of school in the territorial period. *Courtesy Green Valley News*

ABOVE: Tubac park ranger, Cindy Krug, passing out papers. Teachers and students wear authentic costumes of the period funded by the Tubac Historical Society. *Courtesy Green Valley News*

LEFT: Capturing the feel of school in 1885 are Tubac second-graders Alina Fuggiti and Melissa Luna. Each student wears the name tag of an actual student from 1885. *Courtesy Green Valley News*

TUBAC MUSEUM

ABOVE: On display in the Territorial Arizona section is Major General Samuel P. Heintzelman who later served in the Civil War on the Union side. *Courtesy Green Valley News*

BELOW: A Spanish colonial display recalls Tubac's missionaries and military past. *Courtesy Green Valley News*

ABOVE: The Tubac Presidio Museum opened to the public in 1965, seven years after the park was established. *Courtesy Green Valley News*

RIGHT: Tubac's first citizens are remembered in this Native American display. *Courtesy Green Valley News*

ABOVE: Archaeologist and anthropologist, Jack Williams, worked on two excavations in Tubac while completing his doctoral program at the University of Arizona. Here, he takes a group of students on a tour of the Tubac Museum. *Courtesy Green Valley News*

OTERO HALL

ABOVE: The Tubac schoolhouse and visitor center is located in the background. Otero Community Hall with its highly visible tin roof was built by Teófilo Otero in 1914.
Courtesy Bob Johnson Collection, Tubac Historical Society

LEFT: Otero Community Hall served as a place for meetings, dances, church services and additional school rooms. During recent renovations coins were found under the old floor, thrown by dancers.
Courtesy Green Valley News

ROJAS HOUSE

The newest acquisition to the Tubac Presidio State Historic Park is the Rojas House seen in the background of this c. 1920s photo below. An unknown border patrolman is in the foreground while spectators appear to be watching an event near the old presidio ruins or Tubac schoolhouse. Built by Reymundo Rojas c. 1893, it is a typical adobe row house of the Arizona Territorial period.

Luisa Rojas, daughter of Reymundo, lived in the house until her death in 1989. Luisa was born October 10, 1893 in the little tack room (left) behind the main house. She worked as a custodian at the Tubac schoolhouse, located across the road from her home.
Courtesy Herb Lane Collection, Tubac Historical Society

PRINTING PRESS

LEFT & ABOVE: Arizona's first newspaper, *The Weekly Arizonian*, was first published in Tubac on March 3, 1859. This copy (left) was reproduced by park ranger, Wini Chapman, on the original Washington Press shown above. The press was later used in Tombstone to publish the *Tombstone Epitaph*. *Courtesy Tubac Historical Society and Green Valley News*

BELOW: Tubac site of the Arizona Print Shop photographed May 16, 1915 by Robert H. Forbes. The arrow points to the print shop location identified by Sabino Otero. *Courtesy Tumacácori National Historical Park*

LOS TUBAQUEÑOS

ABOVE: The Tubac Jail is believed to be a ring and shackles from the mast of an old ship. How it got to Tubac is unknown, but for many years it was used to detain prisoners until they could be transported to jail in Nogales or Tucson.
Courtesy Stan Benjamin Collection, Tubac Historical Society

ABOVE: Lillie Sheehan and Finn Larkin light the fuse on an old Spanish naval cannon signaling the beginning of the park's Living History program. Sheehan is a founding member of the reenactment group Los Tubaqueños. *Courtesy Tubac Historical Society*

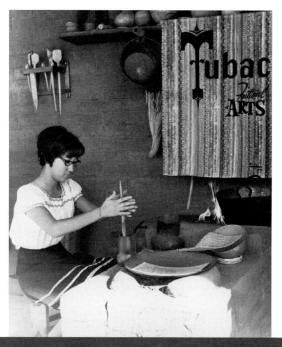

LEFT: October through March, members of Los Tubaqueños demonstrate Spanish colonial life and traditions throughout the park. *Courtesy Tubac Historical Society*

ORIGINAL TUBAC TOWNSITE

ABOVE: Jack S. Williams headed up the Center for Spanish Colonial Archaeology in Tubac in the 1980s & 1990s. Five layers of foundation in the original Tubac townsite can be seen in this photo. *Courtesy Barbara Ruppman Collection, Tubac Historical Society*

RIGHT: Barbara Ruppman, a volunteer with the Center for Spanish Colonial Archaeology, can be seen in the center of the excavation in the early 1990s.
Courtesy Barbara Ruppman Collection, Tubac Historical Society

BELOW: A tour of the original Tubac townsite is lead by Barbara Ruppman, left, and Philip Halpenny.
Courtesy Barbara Ruppman Collection, Tubac Historical Society

TUMACÁCORI NATIONAL HISTORICAL PARK

ABOVE: 1849 sketch of Tumacácori Mission by H. M. T. Powell. His description said: "The church is built chiefly of brick, plastered over. The square tower looks as if it had never been finished. The houses, extending East, are adobe. The church inside is about 90 x 18, painted and gilded with some pretensions to taste. The Altar place under the dome was, of course, more carved, gilded, and painted than anywhere else." Source: *The Sante Fe Trail to California, 1849-1852; The Journal and Drawings of H.M.T. Powell:* Douglas S. Watson, ed., 1931.
Courtesy Tumacácori National Historical Park

ABOVE: Father Eusebio Francisco Kino, the extraordinary Jesuit priest, explorer, cartographer, astronomer, rancher and farmer was the first missionary to set foot in the Santa Cruz River Valley of the Pimería Alta. He established Tumacácori as a mission in January 1691. *"From the Archival Collections, Museum Collections Repository, Western Archeological and Conservation Center, National Park Service"*

BELOW: A French copy of Father Eusebio Kino's original 1705 map of "Passage par Terre a la Californie" dates to 1852. The map was the first to show Baja California as a peninsula and not an island. *Courtesy Tumacácori National Historical Park*

ABOVE: Once again Charles Schuchard is believed to be the artist of this beautiful etching entitled "Ruins of the Mission of Tumacácori," c. 1854. Father Kino established Tumacácori as a mission one day before Guevavi, making it the oldest mission site in Arizona. For many years though, it was a visíta or visiting station of the mission headquarters at Guevavi. During most of those years, it was located on the east side of the Santa Cruz River, and services were held in a small adobe structure built by the Pima inhabitants of the village.
Courtesy Tumacácori National Historical Park

ABOVE: Aerial view of Tumacácori National Monument, date unknown.
Courtesy Tumacácori National Historical Park

LEFT: Jack B. Blake, stationed at Camp Stephen D. Little, circa 1916, poses in front of the Tumacácori Mission. This is a photograph at the main entrance of the mission before repair work began.
Courtesy Tumacácori National Historical Park

BELOW: Tumacácori Mission, showing repair to entrance arch, baptistery window, and second story of the belfry, 1919. *Courtesy Tumacácori National Historical Park*

LEFT: Tumacácori Mission, December 24, 2005 lit by hundreds of luminarias, traditional candles set in sand within a paper bag. *Courtesy Green Valley News*

BELOW: Tumacácori Mission visitors, 1919. *Courtesy Tumacácori National Historical Park*

ABOVE: David Yubeta, park ranger and restoration expert, shines a light on graffiti found in the bell tower of the mission. *Courtesy Green Valley News*

RIGHT: Reconstruction of the Mission c. 1921. *Courtesy Tumacácori National Historical Park*

ABOVE: Tumacácori mortuary chapel in the early 1900s. With a circular design it is approximately sixteen feet in diameter. The roof, possibly intended to be a dome, was never completed. The mortuary chapel would be used when there was a death in a family which didn't live near the mission. *Courtesy Tubac Historical Society*

LEFT: 1930 archaeological excavation on the east side of the Tumacácori Mission. *Courtesy Tumacácori National Historical Park*

LEFT: Workmen trimming and shaping vigas for restoration of the Tumacácori Mission roof, 1922.
Courtesy Tumacácori National Historical Park

RIGHT: Restored Tumacácori Mission as it appears today. *Courtesy Tubac Golf Resort*

BELOW: Workmen making adobe bricks for the Tumacácori Mission wall, February 2, 1934. *Courtesy Tumacácori National Historical Park*

RIGHT: A couple poses on the grounds of the Tumacácori National Monument. In the background is the Convento which was used as a schoolhouse, c. 1925. *Courtesy Tumacácori National Historical Park*

BELOW: Children bearing the body of Christ in a procession during an Easter Ceremony at the Tumacácori Mission, 1936. *Courtesy Tumacácori National Historical Park*

ABOVE: Fiesta de Tumacácori was attended by 3,600 people, December 3, 1972.
Courtesy Tumacácori National Historical Park

RIGHT: Easter Ceremony at the Tumacácori Mission, 1937. *Courtesy Tumacácori National Historical Park*

ABOVE: Manuel and Louise Xavier demonstrate basket weaving, leatherwork and watercolor painting, April 1, 1972. *Courtesy Tumacácori National Historical Park*

LEFT: Father Edmund Dorey poses with a youngster at Tumacácori Mission.
Courtesy Green Valley News

BELOW: Heliodoro Jimenez poses with his clay pots in 1972.
Courtesy Tumacácori National Historical Park

RIGHT: Television crew working on a documentary at Tumacácori, December 1973. *Courtesy Tumacácori National Historical Park*

Residents of Tumacácori Village posed for this photograph in March 1940. Those known: Pina Aldai, Lola Villa, Arturo Villa, José Villa and two of Lola Villa's sons. *Courtesy Tumacácori National Historical Park*

CELEBRATIONS

Enjoy a few memories with these photos of Tubac's past celebrations including the Tubac Festival of the Arts, Anza Days, "How Far, Felipe?" and *El Día de los Muertos* (The Day of the Dead).

In celebration of the arts, the Tubac Festival of the Arts has been held annually since 1959. Each February, local and regional artists make this event one of the premier art festivals in the southwest.

Anza Days, held in October, commemorates the Anza Expedition to San Francisco, California, which departed from Tubac on October 23, 1775. The festival includes events at both the Tubac Presidio State Historic Park and the Tumacácori National Historical Park.

El Día de los Muertos is a traditional celebration in the southwest and Mexico. It was rekindled in Tubac for the first time in over forty years in 1998.

ABOVE: Lori Chavarria, 1990 Tubac Cinco de Mayo Queen.
Courtesy Green Valley News

TUBAC FESTIVAL OF THE ARTS

RIGHT: Cowboy and coyote, 1992. A bit of the old west comes to Tubac.
Courtesy Green Valley News

BELOW AND RIGHT: Vendor tents, 1988 festival. Some years the festival is warm enough for t-shirts and shorts (below). Other years it's cold outside and folks need to bundle up (far right).
Courtesy Green Valley News

ABOVE: Basket making at the Tubac Festival of the Arts. *Courtesy Green Valley News*

BELOW: Take your pick. As the Festival has grown over the years, it has been necessary to close the village to traffic and provide alternate means or getting around. *Courtesy Green Valley News*

LEFT: Herb Appelet of Portal, Arizona, weaving place mats, 1984 festival. *Courtesy Green Valley News*

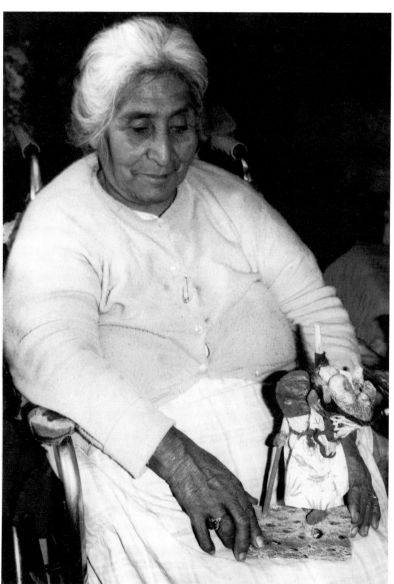

ABOVE: Tohono O'odham craftswoman during the 1970 Tubac Festival of the Arts. *Courtesy Green Valley News*

ABOVE: Braid artisan, 1989 festival.
Courtesy Green Valley News

BELOW: Bob Millar demonstrating water color techqniques, 1984 festival. *Courtesy Green Valley News*

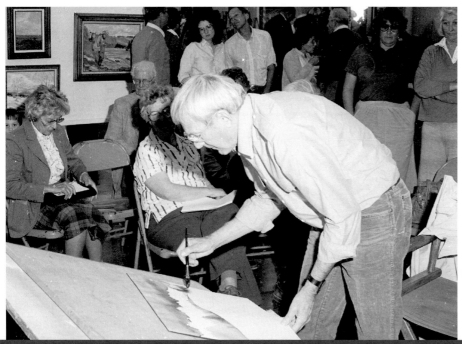

ABOVE: Back-hoe serenade, 1988 festival. *Courtesy Green Valley News*

LEFT: Gloria Moroyoqui de Roque making flowers during the 1998 festival. *Courtesy Green Valley News*

ABOVE: More good food, 1989 festival. *Courtesy Green Valley News*

LEFT: Boy with cone, 1990 festival. *Courtesy Green Valley News*

BELOW: Dancers with rebozos, 1989 festival. *Courtesy Green Valley News*

ABOVE: Littlest folklorico dancers; Maria Otero and partner. *Courtesy Green Valley News*

LEFT: The littlest Mariachis perform in front of the Tubac Center of the Arts. *Courtesy Green Valley News*

BELOW: One of the littlest customers at the 1986 Festival admires the work of artist Cameron Blagg. *Courtesy Green Valley News*

ABOVE: Singers, 1991 festival. *Courtesy Green Valley News*

ABOVE: Two festival visitors grab a bite to eat and admire their purchases. *Courtesy Green Valley News*

ANZA DAYS

ABOVE: Tubac resident, author and historian, Dr. Elizabeth R. Brownell, speaks during the 200th anniversary celebration of the Juan Bautista de Anza Expedition's departure from Tubac on October 23, 1775.

Seated to the left is Arizona Governor Raúl Castro. Standing in the background are Spanish consul general Andres Drake of Los Angeles and Captain Anza in full dress uniform portrayed by Yjinio Aguirre. Will Rogers, Jr., on the right, narrated the departure as descendants of the original expedition participated as honored guests at the event. *Courtesy Tubac Historical Society*

The October 25, 1992 celebration of Anza Days included the dedication of the Juan Bautista de Anza National Historic Trail between Tubac and Tumacácori. Costumed dancers, children and Tubaqueños celebrated in a big way. Susan Wilson in a beautiful Spanish dress rides one of her favorite horses. Local children form a procession past St. Ann's Church and folklorico dancers twirl for delighted spectators. *Courtesy Tubac Historical Society and Green Valley News*

JULY 4, 1961

LEFT: Left to right, Irene Deaton and Cindy Krug during Anza Days 1997. *Courtesy Tubac Historical Society*

RIGHT: Cowboys participating in an Anza Days celebration. *Courtesy Tubac Historical Society*

ABOVE: Reenactors participating in Anza Days during the 1980s. *Courtesy Tubac Historical Society, photograph by Herb Lane*

BELOW: Dick Coler portrays Lt. José Joaquin Moraga during the 1990 Anza Days celebration. *Courtesy Hattie Wilson collection, Tubac Historical Society*

ABOVE: Union and Confederate reenactors participated in the July 4, 1961 event. *Courtesy Tubac Historical Society*

ABOVE: July 8, 1859 is considered to be the first Civil War event in Arizona and took place in Tubac. Sylvester Mowry a southern sympathizer from Rhode Island and Edward Cross, the editor of *The Weekly Arizonian*, held a duel over articles printed in the newspaper. Due to high winds, neither man hit his mark. The participants and spectators retired to the Sonora Exploring & Mining Company's store where a 42-gallon barrel of prime Monongahela whisky was consumed. The event was reenacted during a Fourth of July celebration in 1961. *Courtesy Tubac Historical Society*

RIGHT: Military reenactors are always a popular attraction. *Courtesy Tubac Historical Society*

CELEBRATIONS

"HOW FAR, FELIPE?"

"How Far, Felipe?" was a children's play performed annually to commemorate the trek of Colonel Juan Bautista de Anza II from Tubac to what is now San Francisco. Costumes were handed down year after year and the play, taken from a children's story of the same name by Genevieve Gray, was performed to parents and community members. A highlight for the children was an ice cream cup treat after the show provided by the Tubac Historical Society. *Courtesy Brian and Kathleen Vandervoet of Tubac and Green Valley News*

ABOVE: Marco Bustamonte reads the part of Ruben. *Courtesy Green Valley News*

BELOW: David Jontow, Wendy Ortiz, Claudia Alvarez & Ivan Corona get into costume. *Courtesy Green Valley News*

ABOVE: Tubac students performing "How Far, Felipe?"
Courtesy Green Valley News

RIGHT: Col. Juan Bautista de Anza (Wesley Hansen) peeks from behind his mask.
Courtesy Green Valley News

LEFT: Left to right, Becky Brown plays the part of Aunt María. Hidden behind their masks are Violetta Lopez as Filomena the donkey and Ryan Hansen as Felipe.
Courtesy Green Valley News

ABOVE: Mike McMullen, 7, claps for himself and other performers. *Courtesy Green Valley News*

RIGHT: After the play, the 1986 cast celebrates by dancing.
Courtesy Green Valley News

EL DÍA DE LOS MUERTOS

El Día de los Muertos (The Day of the Dead) is celebrated November 1st or the first Sunday in November. The tradition starts with the cleanup of the cemetery after a summer of monsoon rains and the placing of food and flowers on the graves. Festivities begin after mass with mariachis, folklorico dancers, and most important a chance for family and friends to get together.
Courtesy Tubac Historical Society

November 1, 1998, the tradition of *El Día de los Muertos* was revived in Tubac as the cemetery was turned back to the Tubac Cemetery Preservation Society by Santa Cruz County after forty years.
Courtesy Tubac Historical Society

TUBAC CEMETERY

ABOVE: Graves of Will & Collier Rogers in 1993. *Courtesy Olga Leone*

RIGHT: Simple graves without markers and covered in stones lay beside modern graves in the Tubac Cemetery. *Courtesy Olga Leone*

STARVING ARTIST SALE

ABOVE: Starving Artists Sale in Tubac, May 2-15, 1971. Pictured, left to right, Mary Carry (tacking up pictures), Jean Wilson the teacher in back with the battered hat, Marjorie Nichols, Marion Valentine, Millie Holmquest and artist Eldon Holmquest. *Courtesy Green Valley News*

OLD BUILDINGS WITH NEW FACES

The durability of some of Tubac's oldest homes and buildings can be seen on the pages that follow. Historic structures such as the Pennington House, Charles D. Poston House, Pedro Herreras House, Isidero Otero House, William Lowe House, Little Lowe House, Garrett House, Garrett Store and St. Ann's Roman Catholic Church have survived for generations. They and other historic structures form the unique foundation of today's Tubac.

In the 20th Century well-known notables such as Will Rogers Jr., William Morrow, Dale Nichols, Ross Stefan, Hugh Cabot, Nicholas Wilson and Michael Gibbons, enchanted by the wonderful old adobes, established homes and businesses in these buildings. In so doing, they, restored, enlarged and preserved them for the future.

ABOVE: Possibly the oldest building in Tubac still in use, the Pennington House or Hugh Cabot Studios-Gallery probably dates to pre-territorial days. This building or a portion of it appears in the J. Ross Browne sketch of 1864. *Courtesy Tubac Historical Society*

PENNINGTON HOUSE

RIGHT: Larcena Pennington Page, daughter of an early pioneering family was a young widow when she moved into this old adobe with her younger bothers and sisters in 1864. She had experienced much hardship since her 1858 arrival in Arizona.

In 1860 Larcena was kidnapped by Apaches and left for dead in Madera Canyon. She managed to crawl back to the logging camp where her husband was working, eleven days after the raid. Less than a year later Larcena's husband, John Page, was killed by the Apaches in Cañada de Oro, north of Tucson.

With the 1861 withdrawal of military troops from southern Arizona to fight in the Civil War, Apache attacks became even more frequent. There were very few places of refuge. The Penningtons were forced seek cover at the Patagonia mining camp of Sylvester Mowry. There she gave birth to a daughter, Mary Ann.

By 1864, Tubac was once again one of the safer places in southern Arizona. The presence of the U. S. Military stationed in the old Tubac presidio was reassuring. The Penningtons moved into the old adobe across the plaza.

BELOW: Pennington House, one of the most historic buildings in Tubac, is located on the corner of Calle Iglesia and Placita de Anza. In the 1920s it was owned by Luis and Rosa Lim who had a store, and in 1948 it became the Dale Nichols School of Art. *Courtesy Tubac Historical Society*

Courtesy Virginia Culin Roberts

ABOVE: Dale Nichols lived and taught in Tubac for less than a year, but his legacy lives on. A well known artist from Nebraska by the time he moved to Tubac in 1948, Nichols established an art school in the five old adobe buildings across from St. Ann's. With the help of the GI Bill, WWII soldiers applied as students along with artists from Tucson and the local dude ranches. Unfortunately, some students were not serious about art and soon left. Nichols with financial and personal problems closed the school in 1949 and moved on.
Courtesy Tubac Center of the Arts

ABOVE: The 1948 poster by Dale Nichols advertising the Dale Nichols School of Art.
Courtesy Tubac Historical Society

ABOVE: In 1953 the 17 year-old artist Ross Stefan was creating a sensation in Tucson with his one man shows. In fact he had his first one man show at age 13 in his hometown of Milwaukee, Wisconsin. Inspired by his friend Dale Nichols, he wrote to Nichols in 1955, now living in Antigua, Guatemala, asking about his old adobe in Tubac. With Nichols help Stefan acquired the Tubac art school building and moved in with his young wife Anne. *Courtesy Tucson Museum of Art*

RIGHT: Will and Collier Rogers, Jr. soon became acquainted with Stefan and his wife. This poem, written by Rogers, was recited at the first banquet of the Tubac Chamber of Commerce, February 1, 1961. *Courtesy Tubac Historical Society*

The Tale of Tubac
by Will Rogers, Jr.

It happened in old Tubac
A long, long time ago.
Ross Stefan, on his porch
Was painting a Navajo.

A car drove up, and stopped, and when
The dust had settled down,
Ross could see before him then
A Stranger come to town.

"My name it is Bill Morrow,"
The stranger he did say.
"I want to buy some land
I've money for to pay."

But Ross gave him an argument
"This land's no good, you see.
Forget about the real estate,
And buy some art from me.

"It's the best investment here,
We are artists, due for fame,
These paintings will increase in price,
Once we have made our name."

But Morrow would not be put off,
"Give me no ifs or buts,
I don't know about art,
But I know all about nuts."

"And there are plenty here,
as far as I can see.
Quit painting on that Navajo
And get some land in fee
and just leave the rest to me."

Well, soon the fame of Tubac
Was heard so far away,
They said a second Scottsdale
Was made there every day.

CHORUS
Come back, come back, to Tubac,
Come back, come back; and when
They all come back to Tubac--why
Tubac will rise again--again
Like the might Santa Cruz River,
Tubac will rise again.

LEFT: The Hugh Cabot Studios-Gallery Building looks much as it did 65 years ago. The old adobe has never been plastered or painted.
Courtesy Barbara Ruppman Collection, Tubac Historical Society

Hugh Cabot III, born in Boston, Massachusetts March 22, 1930, died May 23, 2005. Olivia and Hugh Cabot moved to Tubac in 1972. Olivia owned and operated art galleries in New York, Taos, Santa Fe, prior to the Cabot Gallery in Tubac. Cabot chose Tubac because of the intense light, beauty and serenity of the valley. He lived and worked in West Texas, Santa Fe and Taos but he found the light in the Santa Cruz Valley and its extreme beauty inspirational. He was the official artist for the Korean War and these works hang in Washington, D.C. and belong to the American public. Shows of his work have been held at the National Gallery, Washington D.C., the Tate in London, Musée De La Marine in Paris and every major city in the states. One swath of a heavily loaded brush was all he used to depict his subjects. His feeling for light, air and value earned the highly coveted title of American Master Painter and he was ranked among the top 20 painters in America. He spent 34 years in Tubac showing his love for the area and its people through his paintings. His works are collected throughout the world.
Courtesy Olivia Cabot and Green Valley News

POSTON HOUSE

LEFT: It is believed these two adobes belonged to Charles D. Poston. The larger of the two houses was where Poston lived. It was dubbed Territory House, while the small house severed as an office and was known as East House. Shortly after the Gadsden Purchase of 1853, Poston and German mining engineer Herman Ehrenberg arrived in Tubac to check on mining opportunities. Upon visiting the old Salero Mine in the Santa Rita Mountains they saw there was great wealth to be had in Arizona. Investors from the East were found and the Sonora Exploring & Mining Co. headquarters was established at the old Tubac Presidio in 1856. When this picture was taken, the Kimmels had a lovely store called The Tended Earth.
Courtesy Barbara Ruppman Collection Tubac Historical Society

RIGHT: Art and history meet in the studio and home of Michael & Judy Gibbons. Standing next to two ore cars placed on the front porch of their home in honor of Charles Poston, they have renovated and connected the two buildings. A highly gifted landscape artist, Gibbons has numerous awards and has been a member of the Allied Artists of American for more than 20 years. They spend the summer months in their native Oregon. *Courtesy Green Valley News*

BELOW: This advertisement for Territory House Contemporary Watercolors is one of several businesses sponsored by Mr. and Mrs. Douglas Luger. Mr. Luger was a real estate agent and long time resident of Tubac and Tumacacori. Among his properties were the Poston House (dubbed Territory House), above, and he was part owner of Four Winds Ranch. *Courtesy Tubac Historical Society*

PEDRO HERRERAS HOUSE

RIGHT: This quaint adobe next to the Hugh Cabot Studios-Gallery was originally the home of Pedro Herreras, built in 1857. The Herreras family was the owner of the San José de Sonoita land grant on the east side of the Santa Rita Mountains. During the Civil War the building was leased from Herreras for use as a barracks and carpenter shop. In the late 1920s it served as sleeping quarters for Border Patrol agents assigned to Tubac. *Courtesy Barbara Ruppman Collection, Tubac Historical Society*

ABOVE: The Herreras House became the home and studio of Chary Peck in the early 1990s. Shown here at her loom, her textiles and unique southwestern arts and crafts were the highlight of her gallery. *Courtesy Green Valley News*

LEFT: Husband Austin Peck, opened a gallery around the corner in El Presidito. *Courtesy Green Valley News*

ABOVE: Elizabeth R. Brownell (left) with Tubac artist Marjorie Tolkan Nichols. Marjorie was one of Dale Nichols' students in 1948 and they were briefly married. Both left Tubac soon after the Dale Nichols Art School closed, however Marjorie returned in 1959. She moved into the little adobe house next door to the art school known as the Pedro Herreras House. She named her gallery Windsong, a fitting name for Tubac. *Courtesy Green Valley News*

YSIDRO OTERO HOUSE

LEFT: Ysidro Otero, brother of Sabino Otero, was the original owner of the adobe. In 1910 when Southern Pacific train service began between Tucson and Tubac, Otero was able to add a tin roof to the house. *Courtesy Tubac Historical Society*

BELOW: Ann Allen, pictured in front of her home, moved to Tubac with husband John in the early 1970s. *Courtesy Ann Allen Collection, Tubac Historical Society*

ABOVE: One of the older adobes was built by Ysidro Otero c. 1898. It has remained a private home throughout the years. With its distinctive tin roof, it is one of the best preserved adobes in the village.
Courtesy Ann Allen Collection, Tubac Historical Society

LOWE HOUSE

LEFT: The William Lowe family c. 1915. Seven of their nine children are in this photo. Benny the youngest remembers happy days sorting mail and playing in Tubac.
Courtesy Wayne Lowe

ABOVE: Robert Caren, foreman of the Four Winds Ranch, exits from the Tubac post office in the early 1930s.
Courtesy Chary Peck Collection, Tubac Historical Society

LEFT: William Lowe, the second son of Wilhelm Lowe a German immigrant, was forced to move north of the old Tubac presidio when his father's property was lost in the Baca Float No. 3 decision. Besides his duties as the Tubac postmaster, he had a small store, operated a livery business and even sold gas and oil. During his life in Tubac, the Tucson Nogales Highways moved from the east side of his store to a block west on what is now Burruel Street. *Courtesy Tubac Historical Society*

ABOVE: The Lowe House was built by William Lowe in 1904. It served as the Lowe's home, store and Tubac's post office from 1905-1940. The quaint wagon wheel wall creating a beautiful courtyard was added by Collier Rogers.
Courtesy Green Valley News

LEFT: Ramon Quintero, Tubac's mailman, waiting for the mail to be delivered by a Southern Pacific passenger train, 1936. *Courtesy Tubac Historical Society*

ABOVE: The Little Lowe House (built c. 1904) was a private residence for its first six decades, in 1965 it became the home of the Tubac Presidio State Historic Park's first director, Dennis McCarthy and family. In the early 1970s it was the first home of John Montgomery's Artes Alegres, followed by a antique store in the 1980s. Since 1995 it has been the library and headquarters of The Tubac Historical Society.
Courtesy Tubac Historical Society

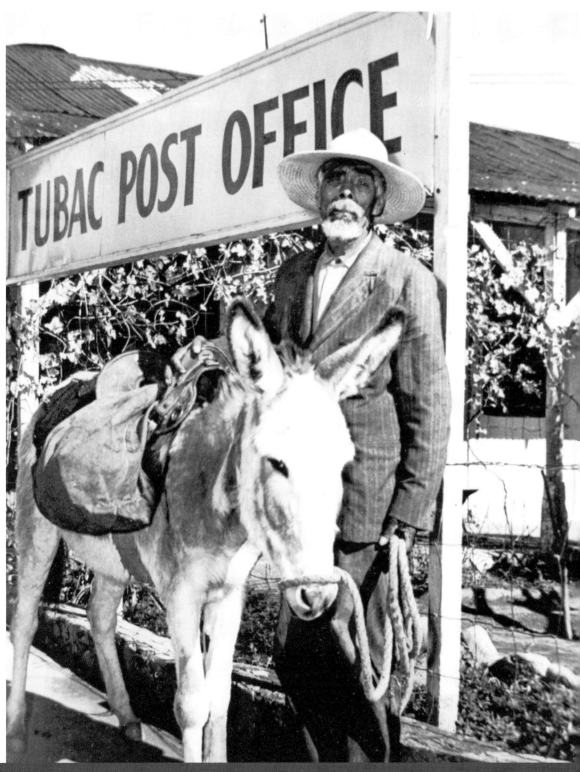

amon Quintero was Tubac's mailman for more than 25 years. ired by William Lowe, he met the Southern Pacific train twice aily delivering and picking up bags from Tucson or Nogales. For any years he carried the bags on his shoulders, sometimes making several trips from the tracks on the east side of the river to the tle post office on the hill. His patient little burro was a gift from illiam Allen the owner of the Kenyon dude ranch who wanted to ake sure his guest received their mail. *Courtesy Tubac Historical Society*

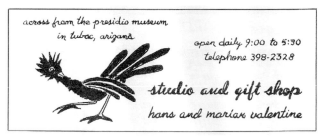

ABOVE: In October 2001, acclaimed wildlife artist Nicholas Wilson and wife Debbe moved into the historic Lowe House. Nick is shown with one of his bobcat "kittens" commissioned by the University of Arizona. The completed ten-foot-tall bronze statue "The Arizona Wildcat Family" is on permanent view in the alumni plaza. Nick's new studio and gallery are located in the Tubac Golf Resort. . *Courtesy Green Valley News*

ABOVE AND LEFT: During the 1970s, the Lowe House became the Valentine Studio and home and continues to remain in the Valentine family. Marion Valentine demonstrates her wax resist watercolor technique on a new painting. Hans Valentine removes the mold from a sand-cast candle during the February 1972 Tubac Festival of the Arts. The historic adobe is now the Los Reyes Gallery and Artist Workshop.
Courtesy Nancy Valentine collection, Tubac Historical Society

ABOVE: William Morrow, owner of the nationwide Morrow's Nut House chain, is shown here with grandson Truly "Bill" Nolen age three and son Jimmy Morrow age five. Morrow with the help of artist Ross Stefan purchased large tracks on land in Tubac including the Lowe House, envisioning a wonderful future for the quiet little village. He was the first major land developer to promote Tubac. A pilot, he often flew his private plane into Tubac, landing on the airstrip built by Mrs. Joanna Shankle.   *Courtesy Scott Nolen*

GARRETT HOUSE

ABOVE: Texas born James T. Garrett, Sr. stands in front of his new two-story house in 1917. It was the first of its type built between Tucson and Nogales and was the first to obtain telephone service. Garrett also built a family run store a few yards from the house.
Courtesy Tubac Historical Society

ABOVE: The Garretts gathered on the front porch for this family photo c. 1920. Father, James T. Garrett with hat is on the right. His wife Harriett is seated to the left. Garrett children include Jessie, Marcella, Jim and Stanford. The identity of the other family members is unknown.   *Courtesy Tubac Historical Society*

LEFT: Stanford Garrett, c. 1920.   *Courtesy Tubac Historical Society*

RIGHT: Jim Garrett, Jr. an outstanding rodeo champion, trick rider and cattle expert, c. 1988. He continued the Texas family tradition as a cattleman.
Courtesy Tubac Historical Society

OLD BUILDINGS WITH NEW FACES

BELOW: The Garrett Store, circa 1926-1929, was headquarters for the newly formed Border Patrol. *Courtesy Leland Crawford Collection, Tubac Historical Society*

LEFT: View of the Garrett Store from the late 1990s. In later years several businesses have occupied the building including Jonathan Shriver's Folk Art Plus and the current Studio 219.
Courtesy Tubac Historical Society

LEFT: José Guaydacan, age 90, worked as a cowboy for the Garretts on their ranch located across the highway on the west side of Tubac. His home was in the historic district of Tubac, east of the old Garrett home and store. Everyday he would ride his big white horse, Gabelon, through the village on his way to and from work. *Courtesy Tubac Historical Society*

RIGHT: Sign identifying the road to the Garrett Ranch on the west side of the highway.
Courtesy Barbara Ruppman Collection, Tubac Historical Society

ABOVE: View looking northeast from the Garrett House. The barn of Bent Youst is on the left, St. Ann's is on the right and the lady in the foreground is believed to be the daughter of Carl White. *Courtesy Tubac Historical Society*

BELOW: This view, c. 1920, is from the second floor of the Garrett House looking east and shows the back of the Garrett Store in the foreground. In the center left to right is St. Ann's Church, the Tubac Schoolhouse, and Otero Hall. Most of the building on the left are now gone. *Courtesy Tubac Historical Society*

GARRET HOUSE - ROGERS

ABOVE: Collier also designed their newly updated living room.
Courtesy Will Rogers Memorial Museum, Claremore, Oklahoma

ABOVE: Will "Bill" Rogers, Jr. and wife Collier moved to Tubac in 1954. They purchased the old Garrett House from Jessie Deubler who had converted it into the Tubac Inn which included a bar and guest rooms. *Courtesy Tubac Historical Society*

RIGHT: Bill and Collier are shown in their recently renovated kitchen designed by Collier. *Courtesy Will Rogers Memorial Museum, Claremore, Oklahoma*

LEFT: Hailing from Tularosa, New Mexico, Collier fell in love with Tubac. She did much to add to the charm of the village including renovation of the Pennington and Lowe houses and adding a small plaza and shrine at the corner of Tubac Road and Burruel Street. She is pictured standing next to the old Garrett Store.
Courtesy Will Rogers Memorial Museum, Claremore, Oklahoma

RIGHT: Bill sits on one of the benches designed by Collier for the little plaza. Just over Bill's shoulder, looking to the southeast, is the north boundary of the Baca Float No. 3. The old Salero Mine and Hacienda de Santa Rita are located in the mountains behind.
Courtesy Will Rogers Memorial Museum, Claremore, Oklahoma

ABOVE: Collier's plaza as it appears today. Bill is seated on one of the benches in the photo above, right.
Courtesy Bob Johnson Collection, Tubac Historical Society

RIGHT: In the 1970s the Rogers built a new home right next door. Today it is the Graham Bell home and gallery. *Courtesy Bob Johnson Collection, Tubac Historical Society*

ST. ANN'S ROMAN CATHOLIC CHURCH

LEFT: This painting of Tubac appeared in an early brochure of Ross Stefan's. Living directly across the road from St. Ann's, it is no wonder that Stefan made St. Ann's the centerpiece of this work.
Courtesy Tubac Historical Society

BELOW: St. Ann's Roman Catholic Church on January 1, 2000, viewed from the Tubac Sculpture Garden looking southwest across the Placita de Anza. The Hugh Cabot Studios-Gallery is on the right.
Courtesy Bob Johnson Collection, Tubac Historical Society

RIGHT: Sketch of Santa Gertrudis Chapel by Phocion B. Way, c. 1858. The chapel was built by Captain Juan Bautista de Anza in the mid 1760s for his troops stationed at the Tubac presidio.
Courtesy Phocion B. Way Diary, Original Manuscript, Arizona State Library Archives and Public Records, History and Records Division, Phoenix, Arizona

BELOW: St. Ann's Roman Catholic Church looking west on Calle Iglesia stands on the foundation of Santa Gertrudis. The Lowe House is on the right.
Courtesy Barbara Ruppman Collection, Tubac Historical Society

OLD BUILDINGS WITH NEW FACES

ABOVE: A grave of an unknown lies in the shade of an old mesquite behind St. Ann's Church c. 1997.
Courtesy Barbara Ruppman Collection, Tubac Historical Society

ABOVE: This roadside shrine once stood next to the old Tucson-Nogales Highway. When the new I-19 freeway threatened to destroy it, Tumacácori resident Josephine Bailey intervened by appealing to the State Department of Transportation. It was moved behind St. Ann's Roman Catholic Church where it has recently been made the focal point of a new reflection garden.
Courtesy Barbara Ruppman Collection, Tubac Historical Society

LEFT: Communion at St. Ann's, 1970s. Seven area children pose on the steps of Saint Ann's after receiving their first communion. Pictured, left to right, front row, Debbie Alegria, John Crandell and Sally Robling. Second row, Joey Jiminez, Gaby Vega, Sarah Trujillo and Frankie Montoya. Third row, Sister Amata Alvey and Father Waldo. *Courtesy Sally Barter*

RIGHT: St. Ann's alter boy walks along the north side of the church, c. 1970s.
Courtesy Tubac Historical Society

ABOVE: St. Ann's Church on a rare snowy day in Tubac. Photo taken from the front porch of the Will Rogers, Jr., home, c. 1965. *Courtesy Will Rogers Memorial Museum, Claremore, Oklahoma*

WHERE THEY LIVED AND WORKED

To an artist, light is everything. Many artists came to Tubac because of the unique qualities of the southern Arizona sun – the way it renders color and shadow. Others came for the camaraderie of creative minds or the high desert beauty of the Santa Cruz Valley.

What is clear is that Tubac has been host to the presence of some of the greatest artists in America and with their arrival Tubac commenced to grow. Combinations of galleries, studios and homes began to line the dirt roads of Tubac. This chapter is devoted to just a smattering of the artists that have made Tubac what it is today. Indeed, this is where they lived and worked....

ABOVE: One of the earliest studios was built by Mortimer and Jean Wilson in 1968. It has been the studio of Lee Blackwell since 1985. *Courtesy Barbara Ruppman Collection, Tubac Historical Society*

ABOVE & RIGHT: Mortimer and Jean Wilson, Jr. moved to Tubac from New York in 1956. For several years they lived on Josephine Bailey's ranch in Tumacácori before building their own place on Plaza Road in the heart of the new Tubac. Mortimer originally worked for the Society of Illustrators while living in the east. His works appeared on the covers of *Cosmopolitan*, *Good Housekeeping* and *Saturday Evening Post*. In Tubac he was able to paint what and when he wanted. Jean Wilson was also a well-known artist when she moved to Tubac. Noted for her still life, trompe l'oeil, and three-dimensional paintings, she was a founding member of the Santa Cruz Valley Art Association.
Courtesy Tubac Center of the Arts and Green Valley News

ABOVE: Born in Colorado, Lee Blackwell's early experience as an artisan began under the tutelage of Ted Egri of Taos, New Mexico. Stretched out beneath one of his original southwestern copper sculptures, Lee rented space from Bunny Hanson at El Sapo when he first arrived in 1982. Since his move to the Wilson studio, his unique copper fountains have grown in fame throughout the southwest. *Courtesy Green Valley News*

ABOVE & LEFT: Irving "Sid" Cedargreen, was a well established businessman in Wickenburg, Arizona when he took up painting in his mid-forties. Buying a starter set of paints and brushes that came with three art lessons, he found he had a natural gift for painting landscapes. On a visit to Tubac in 1957 he stuck up a friendship with Ross Stefan purchasing property from him. The two went into partnership, building the Tubac Art Center on Tubac Road. It would later become the Valley National Bank/Bank One and is now the gallery of Tom Barbre's Cloud Dancer. Cedargreen was one of the founders of the Santa Cruz Valley Art Association.
Courtesy Tubac Center of the Arts and Green Valley News

BELOW: Built in 1980, Virginia Hall's home and studio are located in a quiet cul-de-sac off historic Placita de Anza. *Courtesy Barbara Ruppman Collection, Tubac Historical Society*

ABOVE: Virginia Hall posses with one of her amazing contemporary creations. She prefers to prepare one major collection of paintings a year and presents it to the public as a complete body of work. *Courtesy Green Valley News*

HERE THEY LIVED AND WORKED

Dos Hermanas Gallery, designed by acclaimed Nogales architect Bennie Gonzales is one of the more interesting and most beautiful of the modern buildings in Tubac. It was commissioned by Albert and Trudi Fletcher and opened in 1968. Trudi is known for her paintings in oil and watercolor, as well as silkscreens and batiks. Born in Glendale, California, she began visiting Tubac as early as 1947. She is shown demonstrating her wax on fabric technique for creating original hand painted batik, c. 1970.

Courtesy Tubac Historical Society and Green Valley News

The Dravis Gallery built c. 1969 was located on the corner of Camino Otero and Burruel Street. Shown here in the early 1970s, Earl Dravis surveys his work. He was noted for his sensitive portraits of the Indians of the four corners region. The front of this gallery has decorations saved from the demolition of the old El Conquistador Hotel in Tucson. Wife Faye, a collector of fine Indian jewelry and dolls had her own gallery called the Tubac Doll Shop. After the Dravis' moved on, other business to occupy the building included: Sgt. Grijalva's, Johanna's, Tosh's and currently the De Anza Restaurante & Cantina.

Courtesy Green Valley News and Tubac Historical Society

WHERE THEY LIVED AND WORKED

LEFT & RIGHT: The new Hal Empie Studio was almost ready to open in this 1980 photo. A druggist from Duncan, Arizona, Hal's humorous artistic talent had been enjoyed in the pages of *Arizona Highways* and other publications for many years. However, it was his retirement to Tubac that brought him nationwide recognition for his beautiful oils as reflected in the images hanging in his gallery on Tubac Road.
Courtesy Irene Deaton and Green Valley News

LEFT & BELOW: Artes Alegres, one of Tubac's most beautiful galleries, was built by John Montgomery and the late "Curley" Heiss in 1977. They are pictured in front of their wrought-iron gate leading to a peaceful courtyard. John is known for his desert landscapes, while Curley worked in mosaics made of pot-shards and Italian glass tiles.
Courtesy Green Valley News and John Montgomery

ABOVE: Sally "Bunny" Hanson (left), daughter of Tumacácori rancher Charles "Chay" Day, opened El Sapo in the old Pennington House in partnership with Mal Eaton Tougas, Ann Kennedy and Barbara Morrison in 1970. Mal is pictured below hanging an Indian rug at the entrance of the old adobe.

A couple of years later, in partnership with Lawrence "Coop" Cooper (right), she built a new El Sapo on Camino Otero (below right). El Sapo not only showcases Bunny's artwork, but the works of many other artists and artisans.
Courtesy Irene Deaton and Green Valley News

ABOVE: Luis Martinez, left, and Harwood Steiger work as a team silkscreening fabric designed by Steiger. Steiger and his wife Sophie were living in Alamos, Sonora when William Morrow convinced them to move to Tubac. They built their first studio shop in Morrow's new Tubac Plaza in 1958 and added a 130 foot-long screening room in 1968. *Courtesy Tubac Historical Society*

RIGHT: Wanda Halbwachs, Sophie's niece, came to Tubac to help with the business and continued to run the business after they passed on. The building is currently undergoing major renovation by the new owners. *Courtesy Green Valley News*

LEFT: Shoppers visiting the Steiger Studio. *Courtesy Green Valley News*

Marsha Palmer and Maxine Guy, two talented potters opened their pottery shop in 1970. Marsha, an Ohara Ikebana teacher, designed pottery especially for flower arranging. The building, located at the west end of the village, was originally Bill Loftus' Tubaqueña gas station. Today it is the Zforrest Gallery. In 1971, Maxine moved to her new studio and home and the talented little dynamo, Gwen Frostic from Benonia, Michigan took her place. Renown for her exquisite nature woodblock prints and beautiful books of poetry with every page a visual and textural experience, Gwen would spend a few months in Tubac during the year. Shown here with Laura and John Kerr the four-foot something poet and artist is on the far right. *Courtesy Tubac Historical Society and Green Valley News*

When Maxine Guy built her new home & studio, she included plenty of space for teaching students and taking care of hurt, abandoned or uncared-for wild animals. Her studio, The Potted Owl, was located on Plaza Road across from the Tubac Center of the Arts. Maurice Grossmar (above) cools a newly fired pot. A student (left) hoses down the pot.
Courtesy Green Valley News

Susi and Jarl Hesselbarth were encouraged by their New York friends, Harwood & Sophie Steiger, to move to Tubac in the early 1960s. In 1964 they purchased a building shared by artists El Meyer and Lou Smith. It is now John Ford's Casa de Oro. Jarl, a metal and ceramic sculpture artist, was noted for his whimsical "People Watchers," and fountains.

Susi's beautiful watercolors were soon adorning everything including the tile street signs of Tubac Village. In 1981, Susi was honored by the Santa Cruz Valley Art Association who dedicated the 22nd Tubac Festival of the Arts to her. In the early 1980s New York artist and writer, Olga Leone (below), moved to Tubac and shared space with Susi for a couple of years. Olga soon found that there was a need for local news in Tubac and started the *Tubac Tortilla* newspaper published from 1985-1986.
Courtesy Green Valley News

WHERE THEY LIVED AND WORKED

LEFT AND RIGHT: Seen in a picture from the early 1960s, Alfonso Flores worked for Will & Collier Rogers when they first moved to Tubac. They recognized his artistic talent as a wood carver and helped him to start his own business near their home. Flores' store, La Tienda de Oaxaca is still in business on Will Rogers Lane. In 1991, Alfonso was the featured artist of the annual Tubac Festival of the Arts.
Courtesy Green Valley News and Will Rojers Memorial Museum, Clairmore, OK

LEFT: Today, La Tienda de Oaxaca, located across from The Country Shop, and next to the Graham Bell Gallery, is probably the oldest single owner business in Tubac.
Courtesy Bob Johnson Collection, Tubac Historical Society

RIGHT: Harry Fancher demonstrates his woodworkings techniques for visitors to his Designs in Pine furniture store on Camino Otero. *Courtesy Green Valley News*

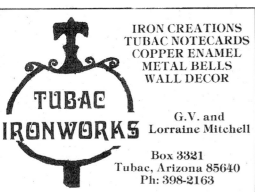

BELOW: Lorraine Mitchell and her late husband "Mitch" moved into the former Harold Wilson home and studio on Plaza Road in 1976. Mitch was a retired iron worker upon arrival in Tubac, but became an artisan of wide repute during the next eleven years. Lorraine has continued the business adding her own artistic talents in watercolor and copper enameling. *Courtesy Barbara Ruppman Collection, Tubac Historical Society and Green Valley News*

HERE THEY LIVED AND WORKED

TUBAC CENTER OF THE ARTS

ABOVE: Tubac Center of the Arts, the heart and soul of the community since October 22, 1972, was the result of ten years of hard work by the Santa Cruz Valley art Association. The building was designed by Tubac artist Harold Wilson a founding member of the Association. *Courtesy Tubac Historical Society*

LEFT: Ted DeGrazia cutting ribbon to open the 11th Annual Festival of the Arts in 1970. Pictured, left to right, Charles Potter, DeGrazia, Eldon Holmquist, Henrietta Itule, William Schaldach, El Meyer, Charles C. Day, Jean Wilson and Mrs. William Schaldach.
Courtesy Santa Cruz Valley Art Association

ABOVE: A member of the Tubac Center of the Arts, Judy Wormser, a gifted artist, is shown here working on a piece of pottery. Judy's home and gallery was located two miles north of Tubac on the old Tucson-Nogales Highway. *Courtesy Green Valley News*

LEFT: Richard Wormser, Judy's husband, a noted western author also wrote for the "Wild, Wild West" television series. He wrote two local books; a humorous cookbook titled *Southwest Cookery, or, At Home on The Range* (pictured in photo) and the always popular book simply titled *Tubac*. *Courtesy Green Valley News*

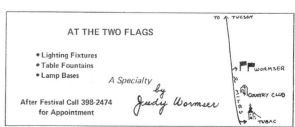

HERE THEY LIVED AND WORKED

ABOVE: In the 1970s, a gifted artist with a love of history moved to Tubac. He was Francis Beaugureau from Chicago. He struck a deal with Valley National Bank of Arizona to paint the military history of Arizona. Eight of his paintings were exhibited in the Phoenix Art Museum.
Courtesy Western Magazine, September 1970.

ABOVE: El Meyer and fellow artist Louis Smith built the second studio in Tubac. Named Los Estudios de Jardin and located at the entrance to the village, it was later studio of the Hesselbarths, and now John Ford. Meyer was elected as the first president of the Santa Cruz Valley Art Association on December 5, 1962. Wife, Hazel was a board member of the Association as well.
Courtesy Green Valley News

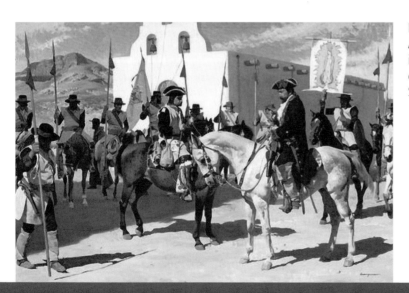

LEFT: This oil painting by Francis Beaugureau, c. 1975, is the perfect example of Tubac's motto "Where Art and History Meet." Here Beaugureau depicts Captain Juan Bautista de Anza and his soldiers departing on their first expedition to establish an overland route to upper California. In the background is the chapel of Santa Gertrudis, site of St. Ann's Church. The original painting is on loan to the Tubac Presidio State Historic Park from the Tubac Historical Society. *Courtesy Tubac Historical Society*

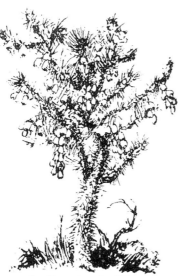

Cholla (with fruits)

ABOVE & RIGHT: In 1958 William Schaldach, already nationally known as an illustrator and editor of *Field and Stream*, moved to Tubac. During his time in Tubac, in addition to continuing his art, he published three highly lauded books featuring his paintings and etchings. A sketch from the 1973 Festival of the Arts brochure appears above.
Courtesy Tubac Center of the Arts

BELOW: The Tubac Center of the Arts embraces all aspects of the arts. Here students attend a harp ensemble. The Tubac Singers are another group that performs regularly.   *Courtesy Green Valley News*

ABOVE: Marjorie Reed, famous for her Butterfield Stage Stop paintings held a spectacular show of her works at the Tubac Art Galleries in 1969. She lived in Amado before moving to Texas Canyon and later Tombstone, Arizona.
Courtesy Green Valley News

RIGHT & BELOW: Harold Wilson, architect of the Tubac Center of the Arts, is shown designing the Masters Meed Medal for the Annual Festival of Arts. The medal is awarded each year to the artist receiving the most votes during the Festival.   *Courtesy Charles D. Lewis, Green Valley News*

RECREATION

The demanding terrain of the surrounding high desert, softened by an abundance of natural resources and beauty, make Tubac one of southwest's top recreational areas.

Today's historic Tubac Golf Resort was formerly the home and ranching empire of Sabino Otero on land granted to his family by the King of Spain in 1789. Originally organized in 1959 as the Tubac Valley Country Club, it was a business venture initiated by real estate developer William Morrow with friend Bing Crosby as Chairman of the Board.

In the 1920s, dude ranches became popular and profitable. Kenyon Ranch, the first dude ranch in the Santa Cruz Valley, provided both recreation and a glimpse of ranching life to wealthy eastern guests.

Rodeos were frequent events at local ranches such as Four Winds, Otho Kinsley's and the roping arena next to Wisdom's. In the 1920s & 30s, polo was the sport of many an eastern dude who introduced it to their western friends.

Softball has had great success in the Tubac area thanks to the hard work and boundless energy of local restaurant owner Herb Wisdom. Teams from all over the United States have participated in games now played on the baseball diamond at the Tubac Community Center.

Tubac is also a key birding and hiking area. Both can easily be accomplished on the four mile Juan Bautista de Anza National Historic Trail between Tubac and Tumacácori. Nearby Madera Canyon, a sky island in the Santa Rita Mountains, is another internationally renowned destination.

ABOVE: Aerial view of the Tubac Valley Country Club, c. 1962. The two silos in the center of the photo identify the historic Otero Land Grant. It is now the Tubac Golf Resort. *Courtesy Tubac Historical Society*

GOLF

ABOVE: The entrance to the Tubac Golf Resort was used in a famous scene from the movie "Tin Cup." The resort was formerly known as the Tubac Valley Country Club. *Courtesy Barbara Ruppman Collection, Tubac Historical Society*

LEFT & BELOW: The 1967 flood of the Santa Cruz River nearly reached the Stables Restaurant. *Courtesy Tubac Historical Society*

ABOVE: One share of the Tubac Valley Country Club owned by Will Rogers, Jr.
Courtesy Tubac Historical Society

LEFT: Otho Kinsley, former owner of the Cow Palace Restaurant, swimming pool, ranch and rodeo arena located in Amado, enjoys dinner with actor John Wayne at the Stables Restaurant, c. 1960.
Courtesy Frank Bertalino, owner Cow Palace Restaurant

ABOVE: The "Tin Cup" lake was added especially for the movie of the same name starring Kevin Costner and Don Johnson. *Courtesy Tubac Golf Resort*

RIGHT: The Otero Ranch house is now one of the rental properties at the Tubac Golf Resort and is often used as the resort's honeymoon suite. *Courtesy Tubac Historical Society*

OPPOSITE: Tubac Valley Country Club golfers in the 1960s. *Courtesy Green Valley News*

DUDE RANCH

ABOVE: Roping a calf on Kenyon Ranch, circa 1940.
Courtesy Kenyon Ranch Collection, Tubac Historical Society

ABOVE: Sign of the first dude ranch in the Santa Cruz Valley, Kenyon Ranch was located directly across the Tuscon-Noglaes Highway (US-89 now I-19) from the Village of Tubac.
Courtesy Kenyon Ranch Collection, Tubac Historical Society

LEFT: Kenyon Ranch looking west, c. 1939.
Courtesy Kenyon Ranch Collection, Tubac Historical Society

RIGHT: Sis and Bill Allen, owners of Kenyon Ranch, strike a pose reminiscent of the Hollywood movies of the day. *Courtesy Kenyon Ranch Collection, Tubac Historical Society*

RIGHT: Horse corral, located below the main ranch house and villas.
Courtesy Kenyon Ranch Collection, Tubac Historical Society

LEFT: Beth Smith Aycock roping a horse in preparation for a trail ride with the dudes, c. 1945.
Courtesy Kenyon Ranch Collection, Tubac Historical Society

RIGHT: Horseback riders at Kenyon Ranch enjoying the wide open spaces of southern Arizona, c. 1940.
Courtesy Kenyon Ranch Collection, Tubac Historical Society

BELOW: Kenyon ranch hands put on a rodeo for the guests.
Courtesy Kenyon Ranch Collection, Tubac Historical Society

BASEBALL

ABOVE: Baseball is a passion for Herb Wisdom. In 2001 he created a baseball diamond behind the Tubac Community Center. Here is the before photo. *Courtesy Herb Wisdom*

LEFT: The infield begins to take shape. *Courtesy Herb Wisdom*

ABOVE: Preparation mean raking a lot of rocks. *Courtesy Herb Wisdom*

RIGHT: Herb Wisdom preparing the field. *Courtesy Herb Wisdom*

ABOVE: A team from Broken Bow, Nebraska takes the field in 2002. *Courtesy Herb Wisdom*

RIGHT: This team came from Houston, Texas to play in Tubac in 2002. *Courtesy Herb Wisdom*

BELOW: At long last, Herb can say "Play Ball." *Courtesy Herb Wisdom*

TUBAC RODEO

Tubac and the surrounding Santa Cruz Valley has a rich tradition of rodeo competition. These photos demonstrate some of the action at the 1987 Tubac Rodeo.

RIGHT: A cowgirl ropes a calf.
Courtesy Green Valley News

BELOW: Speed, agility, and strength are required to win the steer wrestling competition. *Courtesy Green Valley News*

ABOVE & BELOW: Two cowboys try their skill in the team roping competition *Courtesy Green Valley News*

OTHER PLACES OF INTEREST

Considered by many to be an artist colony, Tubac has a unique and diverse collection of businesses that help to support the artists and the arts. Many of the pictures on the following pages were taken by Tubac artist and noted photographer Bob Johnson. They were taken on January 1, 2000 to record Tubac as it was at the beginning of the 21st Century.

Other photos were taken over a two-year period in the late 1990s by local Tubac resident and history buff, Barbara Ruppman.

It is amazing to see how Tubac has changed is less than a decade. To Bob and Barbara we say thanks for the memories.

ABOVE: The Tubac Country Shop, originally the home of the James Garrett family, later the original Tubac Inn owned by Jessie Deubler, and the first home of Will & Collier Rogers, Jr., is located on Will Rogers Lane in the Tubac Plaza. *Courtesy Tubac Historical Society*

RIGHT: Although never an art studio or gallery, the new Tubac Inn was a favorite watering place for many a local Tubac artist and citizen. The Tubac Inn had been in business for five years when the new owners began to feature topless & bottomless dancers in December of 1975. Tubac residents and business people put up a howl of protest, filing a petition claiming "such activity depreciates and lessens the attractiveness of the Tubac Plaza." After much legal wrangling, the Tubac Inn was forced to clean up its act but closed in May of 1976 citing financial problems. *Courtesy Green Valley News*

BELOW: Through the years, the Tubac Inn has had several new names including: Tubac Inn Steak House, The Hideout, Plaza Lounge, and Tubac Jack's Saloon. Today, owner Frank Lagattuta has renamed it the Old Tubac Inn. *Courtesy Tubac Historical Society*

ABOVE: The controversial sign along the Tucson-Nogales Highway that sparked the protest. A flashing red light was placed on the roof of the inn. *Courtesy Tubac Historical Society*

LEFT: Adding to the uproar was this sign on the front door. *Courtesy Tubac Historical Society*

ABOVE & BELOW: In business since 1976, La Paloma de Tubac owned by Cheryl & Bill Green is located on the east side of Tubac in the Old Historic District on Calle Iglesia.

Courtesy Green Valley News and Bob Johnson Collection, Tubac Historical Society

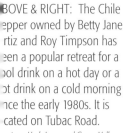

ABOVE & RIGHT: The Chile Pepper owned by Betty Jane Ortiz and Roy Timpson has been a popular retreat for a cool drink on a hot day or a hot drink on a cold morning since the early 1980s. It is located on Tubac Road.

Courtesy Herb Lane and Green Valley News

OTHER PLACES OF INTEREST

LEFT: Pat & Pete Gosha bought an old Titan Missile site on the west side of Tubac and turned it into the Burro Inn with a restaurant and two suites in the 1990s. Pete always wanted a burro and Louie filled the bill. A rather single minded burro, Louie was want to wander off into the desert from time to time, only to be returned by the local cowboys who all knew where he belonged. A second burro named Andrew was acquired to keep Louie company. Pat & Pete kept a big bucket of carrots at the register incase anyone wanted to feed the burros. It is now Crista's Totally Fit.
Courtesy Green Valley News

ABOVE: The Tubac Secret Garden, located in a quiet cul-de-sac in the historic section of the village, is a B&B with gorgeous gardens including a colonnade of roses and a huge bower of wisteria. Popular with local organization and visitors, it is worth a visit just to smell the flowers and enjoy the beauty.
Courtesy Bob Johnson Collection, Tubac Historical Society

LEFT: The Tubac Country Inn was decorated for the holidays in this photo from January 1, 2000. Built in the early 1990s, the B&B is another delightful spot to spend a few days.
Courtesy Bob Johnson Collection, Tubac Historical Society

ABOVE: Left to right are: Bert Fireman and Ricki Rarick of the Arizona Historical Foundation, Mrs. Gay Griffin, Gov. Paul Fannin and Will Rogers Jr. Although Frank Griffin did not live to see the completion of the new museum, it was a proud moment for his wife Gay and friends. As a side note, security was heavy that day, February 2, 1964, as a phone threat against the governor's life had been received.
Courtesy Tubac Historical Society

RIGHT: Frank J. C. Griffin and wife Gay came to Tubac in early 1956 and quickly assessed the historic importance of the little village. They revived Arizona's first newspaper *The Weekly Arizonian* in 1957, republishing articles of historical interest. Inspired by the story of the Tubac presidio, they built El Presidito (above) as a stylized representation of the old Spanish fort in 1958. They acquired several parcels of land on which the ruins of the original presidio stood and formed the Tubac Restoration Foundation, Inc. with the purpose of establishing Arizona's first state park. Other parcel owners, noting the enthusiasm and value of what the Griffins were doing, donated additional lots making the creation of the Tubac Presidio State Historic Park a reality on September 28, 1958. *Courtesy Bob Johnson Collection, Tubac Historical Society*

RIGHT: Griffin called his printing business the *Gun Powder Press*. It was located in the tower.
Courtesy Tubac Historical Society

HIGHWAYS & BYWAYS

Before the Tucson to Nogales Freeway (I-19) was completed in the 1970s the Old Nogales Highway, known as US 89 passed through Tubac, Carmen and Tumacácori.

A century earlier, the road from Tucson to Santa Cruz, Sonora (before there was a Nogales) followed the Santa Cruz River. There was a high road and a low road on either side of the river with crossings at various places including Tubac, Carmen and Tumacácori.

Famed Arizona territorial pioneer Pete Kitchen had another way of describing the road, "Tucson, Tubac, Tumacácori to Tohell." His ranch, El Potrero, was located just north of present day Nogales and was a place of refuge for travelers in the border region.

Today you can enjoy a portion of the old US-89 between Tubac Tumacácori on the East Frontage Road sandwiched between exits 40 and 28. Portions of the road have changed very little. Several businesses and places of interest have been there for generations.

Meanwhile, if you are driving I-19 on your way to Tubac, you will note that it is signed in metric for distance, but miles-per-hour for speed. It is the only Arizona interstate that does not cross into another state. However, it does cross into Mexico becoming Mexico Federal Highway 15.

ABOVE: Abe Trujillo's Old Tumacácori Bar has been in business since the early 1930s. One evening in 1934 John Dillinger is believed to have made a visit robbing the tills of the two slot machines that were sitting on the huge bar. *Courtesy Mary Bingham*

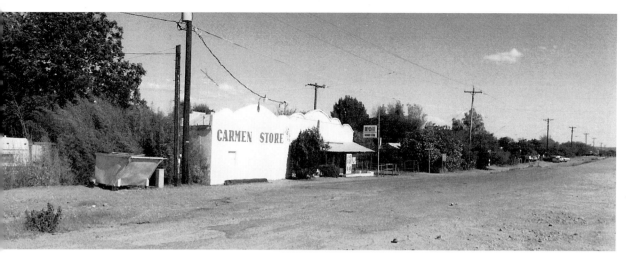

ABOVE: Carmen Store, a landmark since the early 1930s between Tubac and Tumacácori, was owned by Carmen Zepeda (above). She became such a well-known businesswoman in the community, the area was named for her. *Courtesy Barbara Ruppman Collection, Tubac Historical Society and Mary Noon Kasulaitis*

LEFT: Wisdom's Café, a favorite Tumacácori restaurant and bar since 1944 was founded by Howard & Petra (Gomez) Wisdom. It is world famous for its fruit burros and chimichangas. Just look for the two giant chickens guarding the front door.
Courtesy Barbara Ruppman Collection, Tubac Historical Society

BELOW: Alday's, located south of Tubac has long been a popular community hall for weddings, *quinceñeras,* and special occasions.
Courtesy Barbara Ruppman Collection, Tubac Historical Society

RIGHT: Tumacácori Mini Market, owned by the Martinez family, has been in business for over 30 years. *Courtesy Barbara Ruppman Collection, Tubac Historical Society*

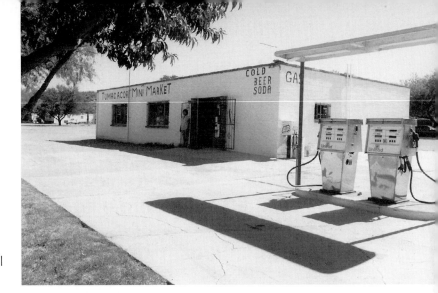

BELOW: Kim Yubeta Designs, located directly across from the Tumacácori Mission, is the place to find unique hand crafted jewelry. Kim's husband David is a ranger at the Tumacácori National Historical Park. *Courtesy Barbara Ruppman Collection, Tubac Historical Society and Green Valley News*

LEFT: Entrance to the always peaceful Rancho Santa Cruz.
Courtesy Green Valley News

BELOW: Main ranch house at Rancho Santa Cruz in Tumacácori.
Courtesy Green Valley News

ABOVE: Rock Corral Ranch, 1931. Ranch foreman Nacho Flores stands near rock in the right foreground. *Courtesy Jean England Neubauer*

LEFT: Jean England Neubauer in front of the Santa Cruz Chili factory, 1990s. The business was founded by Jean's parents Gene and Juliet. Gene England came to Arizona from Texas in 1931 and purchased the Rock Corral Ranch, and passed on to her. *Courtesy Green Valley News*

BELOW: Rock Corral Ranch in Tumacácori was named for this large rock corral, the ruins of which are still visible. *Courtesy Dan Di Sarno*

A

Acuña home 16
Aguirre, Yjinio 49
Alamos, Sonora 86
Aldai, Pina 42
Alday's 113
Alegria, Debbie 76
Allen, John & Ann 65
Allen, William "Bill" & Sis 67, 102
Allied Artists of America 63
Alvarez, Claudia 53
Alvey, Amata (Sister) 76
Amado, Arizona 96, 99
American Master Painter 62
Andrade, Cayetano 15
Andrade, Ynez 15
Annual Tubac Festival of the Arts .... (see Tubac Festival of the Arts)
Antigua, Guatemala 61
Anza Days 6, 43, 49-51
Anza Days - "How Far, Felipe?" 43, 52-54
Anza Expedition 6, 43, 49, 94
Anza Trail 16
Anza, Juan Bautista de (Capt.), (Col.) 6, 7, 24, 49, 52, 53, 75, 94
Apaches 60
Appelet, Herb 45
archaeological excavation 28, 33, 37
Arizona Historical Foundation 111
Arizona Print Shop 31
Arizona territorial period 11, 30
Arizona's first state park 23, 111
Artes Alegres 66, 84
Aycock, Beth Smith 103
Aztec Mining District 12, 14

B

Baca Float No. 3 ..... 12, 15, 66, 73
Bailey, Josephine 76, 79
Barbre, Tom 81
Barnacastle, Bob 26
barrio de Tubac 21
baseball 104-105

Beattie, Samuel H. 25, 26
Beaugureau, Francis 94
Bell, Graham 73
Bernett, Mr. 19
Blackwell, Lee 78, 80, 85
Blagg, Cameron 48
Blake, Jack B. 35
Border Patrol 64, 70
Broken Bow, Nebraska team 105
Brown, Becky 54
Browne, John Ross 7, 14, 59
Brownell, Elizabeth R. (Dr.) 49, 64
Burro Inn 110
Burruel Street 21, 22, 66, 73, 83
Bustamonte, Marco 53

C

Cabot Gallery 62
Cabot, Hugh III & Oliva 59, 62
California 6, 94
Calle Iglesia 17, 60, 75, 109
Camino Otero 83, 85
Camp Stephen D. Little, Nogales, Arizona 35
Canada de Oro, Arizona 60
Cantina 21
Caren, Robert J.; Chris 18, 20, 66
Carmen Store 113
Carmen, Arizona 112
Carry, Mary 58
Casa de Oro 89
Castro, Raúl (Governor) 49
Cedargreen, Irving "Sid" 81
Celebrations 39-40, 43-58
Center for Spanish Colonial Archaeology 33

Chapman, Wini 3
Charles D. Poston House 5
Chavarria, Lori 4
Chile Pepper 10
Cinco de Mayo Queen 4
Civil War 7, 28, 51, 60, 6
Cloud Dancer 8
Coenen, Ana Marie 1
Coler, Dick 5
Company B, 340th Field Artillery 1
Cooper, Lawrence "Coop" 8
Corona, Ivan 5
Costner, Kevin 10
Country Shop (The) 90, 10
Cow Palace Restaurant 9
Crandell, John 7
Crista's Totally Fit 11
Crosby, Bing 9
Cross, Edward 5

D

Dale Nichols School of Art 60, 61, 6
Day, Charles "Chay" 85, 9
De Anza Restaurante & Cantina 8
Deaton, Irene 5
DeGrazia, Ted 9
Designs in Pine 9
Deubler, Jessie 72, 10
Dillinger, John 11
Doña Ana County, New Mexico Territory ....
Dorey, Edmund (Father) 4
Dos Hermanas Gallery 8
Drake, Andres 4
Dravis Gallery 8

Travis, Earl & Faye 83
Dude ranch 97, 102
Duncan, Arizona 84

E

East Frontage Road 22, 112
East House 63
Easter Ceremony 39, 40
Egri, Ted 80
Ehrenberg, Herman 63
El Conquistador Hotel 83
El Dia de los Muertos 43, 55-56
El Potrero 112
El Presidito 22, 64, 111
El Sapo 80, 85
El Torreón Ranch 15
Elizabeth R. Brownell Library 25
Empie, Hal 84
England, Gene & Juliet "Judy" 116
Ensley, Marie 25

F

Fancher, Harry 91
Fannin, Paul (Gov.) 111
Festival of the Arts ..... (see Tubac)
Field and Stream 95
Fiesta de Tumacacori 40
Figueroa, Jose María 26
Fireman, Bert 111
First printing Press 31
First Spanish land grant 10
First telephone service 69
Fletcher, Albert & Trudi 82
Flores, Alfonso 89
Flores, Nacho 116
Folk Art Plus 70
Forbes, Robert H. 16, 17, 31
Ford, John 89, 94
Four Winds Ranch 18-19, 63, 66, 97
Franciscans 23
Frostic, Gwen 87
Fuggiti, Alina 27

G

Gadsden Purchase 7, 63
Garrett House & Store 22, 59, 69-73
Garrett Ranch 70
Garrett, James T., Sr.; Harriett; Jessie; Jim Jr.; Marcella; Stanford 69, 107
Gastellum, Luis Acuña 16
Gastelum, Jimmie; Louis 25
GI Bill 61
Gibbons, Michael & Judy 59, 63
Glassman hotel 9
Glassman, Henry 26
Glendale, California 82
Goldberg, Issac 26
Gonzales, Bennie 82
Gosha, Pete & Pat 110
Graham Bell Gallery 90
Gray, Genevieve 52
Green, Bill & Cheryl 109
Griffin, Frank J. C. & Gay 23, 111
Grossman, Maurice 88
Grosvenor, Horace 6
Guaydacan, José 70
Guevavi Mission 6, 23, 34
Gun Powder Press 111
Guy, Maxine 87, 88

H

Hacienda de Santa Rita 7, 12, 14, 73
Hal Empie Studio 84
Halbwachs, Wanda 86
Hall, Virginia 81
Halpenny, Philip 33
Hansen, Ryan 54
Hansen, Wesley 53
Hanson, Sally "Bunny" 80, 85
Harper's New Monthly Magazine 7
Harwood Steiger's Factory 22
Havier, Manuel and Louise 41
Heintzelman, Samuel P. (Major General) 6, 28
Heiss, "Curley" 84
Herreras, Pedro 64
Hesselbarth Gallery 22
Hesselbarth, Jarl & Susi 89, 94, 114
Hideout (The) 108
Hinton's Handbook to Arizona, 1877 14
Holmquest, Eldon & Millie 58, 92
Hugh Cabot Studios-Gallery 7, 16, 59, 64, 74
Huston, Texas team 105

I

I-19 freeway 76, 102, 112
Illustrations:
    "A Tour Through Arizona" 7
    "Early View of Tubac and the Santa Rita Mountains" 8
    "Hacienda de Santa Rita Mining Company" 14
    "Ruins of the Mission of Tumacacori" 34
    "Valley of the Santa Cruz" 8
Illustration: Sketch of Tumacacori Mission 34
Itule, Henrietta 92

J

J. D. Halstead Lumber Co. 1
Jesuit mine 1
Jesuit missionary 6, 23, 3
Jimenez, Heliodoro 4
Jiminez, Joey 7
Johanna's 8
Johnson, Bob 10
Johnson, Don 10
Jontow, David 5
Juan Bautista de Anza National Historical Trail 50, 9

K

Kearns, Mr. 1
Kennedy, Ann 8
Kenyon Ranch (dude) 67, 97, 102-10
Kerr, John & Laura 8
Kim Yubeta Designs 1
King family brand ....
King of Spain ....
King Ranch 2
King, Joseph (I) 12, 2
King, Joseph (II) 1
King, Margarita Andrade ....
Kino, Eusebio Francisco (Father) 6, 23,
Kinsley, Otho 97,
Kitchen, Pete 1
Krug, Cindy 27,

L

La Paloma de Tubac 1
La Tienda de Oaxaca ....
Lagattuta, Frank 1

Larkin, Finn 32
Leone, Olga 89
Lim, Luis and Rosa 60
Little Lowe House 59, 66
Living History program 32
Loftus, Bill 87
Lopez, Violetta 54
Los Estudios de Jardin 94
Los Reyes Gallery and Artist Workshop 68
Los Santos Angeles de Guevavi ....(see Guevavi)
Los Tubaqueños 31
Lowe House 16, 17, 22, 66-68, 73, 75
Lowe, Benny 66
Lowe, Oralia; Roberto 25
Lowe, Wilhelm 66
Lowe, William 66, 67
Luger, Douglas 63
Luna, Melissa 27

M

Madera Canyon 60, 97
Main Street 21, 22
Maps:
    Passage par Terre a la Californie 34
    Santa Rita Township 14
    Tubac 1766-1767 24
Marquez de Andrade, Mariana 15
Martinez family 114
Martinez, Luis 86
Martinez, Theresa 25
Masters Meed Medal 96
McCarthy, Dennis 66
McMullen, Mike 54
Mercer, T. Lillie 13, 25

Mexico Federal Highway 15 112
Meyer, El & Hazel 89, 92, 94
Millar, Bob 46
Mission San José de Tumacácori ....(see Tumacacori Mission)
missions 6
Mitchell, Lorraine & "Mitch" 91
Montgomery, John 66, 84
Montoya, Frankie 76
Moraga, Maria 25
Moroyoqui de Roque, Gloria 46
Morrison, Barbara 85
Morrow, William; Jimmy 23, 59, 68, 86, 97
Morrow's Nut House chain 68
Mowry, Sylvester 51, 60
Musée De La Marine, Paris 62

N

National Gallery 62
National Register of Historic Places 25
Neubauer, Jean England 116
New Spain 23
New York 62, 79, 89
Nichols, Dale 59, 61, 64
Nichols, Marjorie Tolkan 58, 64
Nogales jail 15
Nogales, Arizona 13, 15, 17, 32, 67, 69, 82, 112
Nogales, Sonora, Mexico 8
Nolen, Truly "Bill" 68

O

Ochoa, Jesus; Victoria 25
Old Historic District 109
Old Nogales Highway 112
Old Tubac Inn 108
Old Tumacacori Bar 112

Olivas, Anita; Felix	25
Original Tubac Town site	33
Ortiz, Betty Jane	109
Ortiz, Wendy	53
Otero Community Hall	10, 21, 22, 23, 29, 71
Otero family brands	10
Otero land grant	10, 11
Otero Ranch house	101
Otero, Joe	25
Otero, Maria	48
Otero, Sabino	11, 25, 31, 64, 97
Otero, Teofilo	29
Otero, Toribio de (Don)	10, 11
Otero, Ysidro	65

P

Pachecko, Dolores	26
Page, John	60
Page, Mary Ann	60
Palmer, Marsha	87
Parrish, Pearl	25
Patagonia mining camp	60
Peachey family	12
Peck, Austin & Chary	64
Pedro Herreras House	59, 64
Pennington House	17, 22, 59, 60-62, 73, 85
Pennington Page, Larcena	16, 60
Penningtons	60
Peters, James	26
Pie Allen's stand	16
Pima inhabitants	34
Pima Rebellion	23
Pimería Alta	6, 34
Placita de Anza	60, 74, 81

plaza and shrine	73
Plaza Lounge	108
Plaza Road	79, 88, 91
Poston House	(see Territory House)
Poston, Charles Debrille	6, 7, 14, 17, 63
Potted Owl (The)	88
Potter, Charles	92
Powell, H. M. T.	34
Presidio de San Igancio de Tubac	(see Tubac Presidio)
Pumpelly, Raphael	6
Purple Garlic (The)	85

Q

Quintero, Ramon	66, 67

R

Ramirez de King, Trinidad	12
ranchería	6
Rancho Santa Cruz	115
Rarick, Rick	111
recreation	97-106
Reed, Marjorie	96
restoration	38
Rio de Tubac	24
Roads (caminos) - Altar Valley, San Xavier del Bac, Sonitac, Tumacácori	24
roadside shrine	76
Robling, Sally	76
Rock Corral Ranch	116
rodeo	97, 103, 106
Rogers, Will "Bill", Jr. & Collier	23, 49, 57, 59, 61, 66, 72-73, 77, 90, 99, 107, 111
Rogers: "The Tale of Tubac"	61
Rojas House	9, 23, 30
Rojas, Luisa; Reymundo	30
Rosenburg, Adeline; Stella	25
Ruppman, Barbara	33, 107

S

Salcido, Angelita 25
Salero Mine 7, 12, 14, 63, 73
Salero Ranch 14
Salero road 12
San Cayetano de Tumacácori ..... (see Tumacácori Mission)
San Francisco, (Alta) California 43, 53
San Igancio de Tubac Presidio ..... (see Tubac Presidio)
San Jose de Sonoita land grant 64
San Xavier del Bac 6, 23
Santa Cruz Chili Factory 116
Santa Cruz County 56
Santa Cruz County constable 15
Santa Cruz River 23, 34, 98
Santa Cruz Valley 34, 62, 78, 97, 102, 106
Santa Cruz Valley Art Association 79, 81, 89, 92, 94
Santa Cruz, Sonora 112
Santa Gertrudis Chapel 7, 75, 94
Santa Rita Mountains 26, 63, 64, 97
Saturday Evening Post 79
Schaldach, William & Mrs. 92, 95
Schuchard, Charles 8, 34
Sgt. Grijalva's 83
Shankle, Joanna 68
Sheehan, Lillie 32
Shriver, Jonathan 70
Sinohui, Miguel B. 21
Sinouhi, Isabel; Lucinda; Mercedes 25
Smith, John T. 26
Smith, Louis "Lou" 89, 94
Society of Illustrators 79
soldados de cuera 23
Sonora Exploring and Mining Co. 7, 51, 63
Southern Pacific train 65, 66, 67
Spanish & Mexican colonial period 11
Spanish colonial display 28
Spanish colonial life and traditions 32
Spanish consul general of Los Angeles 49
Spanish frontier 23
St. Ann's Parrish Hall 22
St. Ann's Roman Catholic Church 16, 17, 21, 22, 25, 50, 59, 61, 71, 74-77, 94
St. Joseph's Cemetery 12
Stables Restaurant 98, 99
Stage Coach 8
Starving Artist Sale 58
State Department of Transportation 76
Steel, Mr. 19
Stefan, Ross & Anne 59, 61, 68, 74, 81
Steiger Studio 86
Steiger, Harwood & Sophie 86, 89
storms of 1914-1915 17
Studio 219 70

T

Taos, New Mexico 62, 80
Tapia, María Amparo 13
Tate Gallery, London 62
teacherage 25
Tended Earth (The) 63
Territorial Arizona 28
Territorial Tubac 7
Territory House 22, 63
Texas Western Railroad Survey 8
The Day of the Dead 43, 55
The Weekly Arizonian 31, 51, 111
Timpson, Roy 109
Titian Missile site 110

Tohono O'odham craftswoman ... 45
Tombstone Epitaph ... 31
Tombstone, Arizona ... 31, 96
topless & bottomless dancers ... 108
Tosh's ... 83
Tougas, Mal ... 85
Trujillo, Abe ... 112
Trujillo, Sarah ... 76
Truman Mining District ... 12
Tubac ... 6, 7, 13, 97
Tubac Art Center ... 22, 81
Tubac Art Galleries ... 96
Tubac Cemetery ... 22, 56
Tubac Cemetery Preservation Society ... 56
Tubac Center of the Arts ... 48, 88, 92, 93, 95, 96
Tubac Chamber of Commerce ... 61
Tubac class of 1929 ... 25
Tubac Community Center ... 97, 104
Tubac Country Inn ... 110
Tubac Doll Shop ... 83
Tubac Festival of the Arts ... 43, 44-48, 68, 89, 90, 92, 95, 96
Tubac Golf Resort ... 10, 68, 97, 98-101
Tubac Golf Resort - "Tin Cup" ... 98, 101
Tubac Historical Society ... 25, 27, 52, 66, 94
Tubac in 1970 ... 22
Tubac in the 1920s ... 21
Tubac Inn (new) ... 108
Tubac Inn (original) ... 72, 107
Tubac Inn (The) ... 22
Tubac Inn Steak hose ... 108
Tubac Ironworks ... 91
Tubac Jack's Saloon ... 108
Tubac Jail ... 32
Tubac mailman ... 67

Tubac Plaza ... 86, 107
Tubac post office ... 16, 66
Tubac postmaster ... 66
Tubac Presidio ... 6, 7, 22, 24, 60, 63, 66, 75, 111
Tubac Presidio Museum ... 23, 28
Tubac Presidio State Historic Park ... 23, 24-33, 43, 66, 94, 111
Tubac Restoration Foundation, Inc. ... 111
Tubac Road ... 73, 81, 109
Tubac Rodeo (1987) ... 106
Tubac School District ... 26
Tubac Schoolhouse (Old) ... 16, 17, 21, 22, 25-27, 29, 30, 71
Tubac Sculpture Garden ... 74
Tubac Secret Garden ... 110
Tubac Singers ... 95
Tubac Tortilla ... 89
Tubac Valley Country Club ... 97, 98, 99, 101
Tubac Valley Country Club & Estates ... 22
Tubaqueña gas station ... 87
Tucson presidio ... 23
Tucson, Arizona ... 11, 32, 60, 61, 65, 67, 69, 83, 112
Tucson-Nogales Highway ... 16, 21, 22, 66, 76, 93, 102, 112
Tully & Ochoa Store ... 16
Tumacacori Mini Market ... 114
Tumacácori Mission ... 6, 23, 34-42, 114
Tumacacori Mountains ... 26
Tumacacori National Historical Park/National Monument ... 23, 34-42
Tumacacori Village residents ... 42
Tumacacori, Arizona ... 18, 50, 76, 79, 85, 97, 112, 113, 115
Tyndall Mining District ... 12, 14

U

U. S. Army ... 7, 13
U. S. Military ... 60
Union ... 28

Union and Confederate reenactors 51
University of Arizona 28, 68
Urrutia, Josef de 24
US-89 highway 102, 112

V

Valdez, Refugio 25
Valentine Studio 68
Valentine, Marion & Hans 58, 68
Valley National Bank/Bank One 81, 94
Vega, Gaby 76
Vega, Maria; Rosalia 25
Villa, Arturo; Jose; Lola 42
Village of Tubac 102
visita 34

W

Waldo (Father) 76
Washington Press 31
Way, Phocion B. 75
Wayne, John 99
White, Carl 71
Wickenburg, Arizona 81
Will Rogers Lane 90, 107
William Lowe House 59
Williams, Edwin P. 25
Williams, Jack S. 28, 33
Wilson Studio 80
Wilson, Harold 91, 92, 96
Wilson, Mortimer & Jean 58, 78, 79, 92
Wilson, Nicholas 59, 68
Wilson, Susan 50
Wilson: "The Arizona Wildcat Family" 68
Windsong Gallery 64
Wisdom, Herb 97, 104-105

Wisdom, Howard & Petra 113
Wisdom's Café 113
World War I (WWI) 13
World War II (WWII) 61
Wormser, Richard & Judy 93
Wormser: "Wild Wild West" 93
Wrightson, William 6, 12

Y

Youst, Bent 71
Ysidero Otero House 59
Yubeta, David & Kim 37, 114

Z

Zepeda, Carmen 113
Zforrest Gallery 87

Brasher Real Estate

Brasher Real Estate provides a variety of services in residential re-sales, new home sales, commercial properties, ranches and large estates. It also has an active property management division. In 2006 the company had six offices serving the Valley. Its new home sales division represents Barrio de Tubac: Trails Head, Santiago, Embarcadero, and Sentinel Hill; Alamos in Green Valley; and The Tubac Golf Resort. Re-sale offices are located in the Village of Tubac, Green Valley and the Tubac Golf Resort.

Brasher Real Estate has been serving the Tubac Valley since 1986 however the roots of its owners go much deeper into Arizona's history than that. Brother and sister, Gary and Jacque Brasher, both company principals, are fifth generation Arizonians. Partner, Zachary Freeland, was born near Nogales and later served as mayor of Sahuarita, Arizona. Zach now lives in Barrio de Tubac. Another owner, Carl Bosse moved to Tubac in 1967 and has lived in Southern Arizona since. His father, Richard, was co-founder of the Santa Cruz Valley Citizen's Council and served 15 years as its president.

The Bosque at the Barrio

The town homes surround a mature mesquite bosque and charming water feature.

Anza National Trail

Barrio residents on a four mile hike to Mission Tumacacori.

Sentinel Hill

A view of the Santa Cruz Valley from one of the 44 home sites within this classic community.

Parque de Anza

A place for the community to come together.

Santiago

The Barrio's Flagship Community, Santigio, located within a mature mesquite forest.

Cielito Lindo
A view of this town home community from near the Anza National Historical Trail.

Embarcadero
Construction underway on the 180 unit Embarcadero Town Home complex.

Entrance to Barrio de Tubac

Dorn Homes

For over 33 years Dorn Homes has been creating custom homes and luxury planned communities in Arizona. Dorn has been ranked the "#1 Custom Home Builder" in southern Arizona for 4 years in a row by *Inside Tucson Business*, and was the only homebuilder to receive the Better Business Bureau's

highest honor, "The Ethics in Business Award." Dorn Homes, owned by David and Ellen Grounds, consists of an exemplary group of partners including local residents Julie Grounds, Lorin Jacobson and Ellen Carpenter who are committed to celebrating the unique history and personality of Tubac in the distinctive homes and communities they have overseen.

Ellen Carpenter, Lorin Jacobson and Julie Grounds of Dorn Homes

David and Ellen Grounds, Dorn Homes

Dorn Homes and its subsidiary Tubac Homes are leading the Renaissance in Tubac with the development of over seven celebrated communities that each combine historical architecture with the integration of modern Building Sciences and conveniences.

Tubac Golf Resort

In 1787, on behalf of King Charles III of Spain, Don Toribio de Otero was granted a home site and four farming lots, just north of the village of Tubac. In return, Otero was obliged to plant fruit trees and other crops to supply soldiers at the Tubac Presidio with food and horses.

This 400-acre land grant formed the core of what later became the largest cattle empire in Arizona and ultimately, the Tubac Golf Resort.

Unrelenting attacks by Indians, Mexico's independence from Spain in 1821, and occasional years of drought, caused the little town of Tubac to be abandoned several times. The Gadsden Purchase decreed this area of Arizona part of the United States in 1853. Toribio Otero's grandson, Sabino, became head of the family in 1863 at the age of nineteen. During the American Civil War, Tubac briefly came under the control of the Confederacy, but the absence of protective troops invited fierce waves of Indian attacks. For safety, Sabino took his family across the border to Buzani, Sonora; it was here that he became interested in raising cattle. Returning to Arizona in 1870, Sabino began to build up his herds, and to supply the local garrisons established to fight Geronimo and the Apaches. Sabino's partnerships and connections on both sides of the border, earned him the title of "Cattle King of Arizona".

Sabino Otero

Sabino's younger brother, Teofilo, inherited this vast estate, but a series of droughts and increased competition made the cattle business less and less appealing. Teofilo sold off all of the ranches except the old family 400-acre land grant. The ranch changed hands several times after Teofilo's death in 1941. Among its owners were Joanna Shankle Davis, an early aviator who flew in the famed Woman's Powder Puff Air Derby in 1929, and a colorful local banker and real estate baron, Wirt Bowman. In 1959, a group of businessmen acquired the Otero Ranch and, with the late great Bing Crosby as Chairman of the board, began the organization, which today is, the Tubac Golf Resort. Recently, the golf resort was a feature location in the making of the motion picture "Tin Cup". Currently, Ron Allred, developer of Telluride, Colorado owns the resort.